YOUR
FINANCIAL REVOLUTION

The Power of Provision

GARY KEESEE

TABLE OF CONTENTS

INTRODUCTION

The title of this book may seem like a no-brainer, something that is an obvious statement of fact. I mean, who would argue its merit? I think we all would agree that having provision, provision for the things we need in life, is essential. Yet so many do not have the provision they need. Many, in fact, are fighting to have just enough to survive. They live lives of slavery to the bills and debt that seem to have no end. Instead of living their dreams, they are living in a state of despair, overwhelmed with the dread of going to a job they hate, and worst of all, living with no meaningful purpose.

A recent study says that 48% of Americans bring home $31,561 a year, or $2,630 or less a month,[1] and 40% of the population cannot write out a check for $400 without first planning for it.[2]

Can you imagine the stress of having to watch every penny you spend, hoping to just make it to the next payday week after week, month after month, with no end in sight? Instead of getting ahead, you find that you are falling further into debt with no way out. I can imagine it, because that is how I lived for nine long years; and it was not my imagination either. It was very real.

---

1 https://howmuch.net/articles/how-much-americans-make-in-wages

2 https://www.cnbc.com/2018/05/22/fed-survey-40-percent-of-adults-cant-cover-400-emergency-expense.html

The Shame of Lack

My wife, Drenda, and I got married and hoped to start an amazing life, but we found ourselves in debt and living a life of financial stress. In just a few short years, we found ourselves with 10 maxed out and canceled credit cards; three finance company loans at 28% interest; car payments on two junk cars, both with over 200,000 miles on them; IRS liens; and numerous other debts we could not pay. We owed our parents thousands of dollars, to the point that they stopped loaning us money.

It's not like we set out to destroy our lives with debt; we were simply trying to survive. As crazy as this sounds, I was in the financial field helping people with their insurance and investment needs. I was being paid on a 100% commissions' basis from the sales I would make, but the commissions were never enough. We kept hoping that the business would pick up, but the weeks turned into years with no change.

Eventually, after nine long years of relying on debt to pay the bills, we exhausted every possible means of borrowing money we could think of. We pawned almost everything of value we could find, and the stress of living in that financial quagmire began to take a serious emotional toll on me and my family.

I developed panic attacks and was put on antidepressants, which really did not help and caused their own set of serious side effects. I was also told by my doctors that I would have diabetes based on blood sugar issues I was having.

Worse than my medical issues was the fear that overtook my life to the point that I was even afraid to leave my house. My world was closing in around me with a hellish, tormenting dread that was paralyzing! We were behind on all our bills, and every month, it was a challenge to figure out which one we had to pay and which one we could skip until next month.

I suppose one of the most debilitating aspects of the financial mess we lived in was the shame I felt. Fear would grip me every time I used a credit card hoping it would work one more time. I found myself constantly making up excuses, lying really, to the bill collectors that called on an almost daily basis. Probably the toughest thing to endure was seeing my beautiful family doing without the things they needed, which caused an ache in my soul. To be honest, I felt like a failure almost every day as I dealt with one problem after another.

This financial chaos was not a blimp on the radar, a moment in time. This went on for nine long years!

In case you are wondering, yes, we were in church every week. I had a degree in theology and business and had attended one year of Bible school. I was baptized in the Holy Spirit, and I loved God, but something was terribly wrong. I knew that, but what? The stories that I read in the Bible were just not happening in real life.

We were going to a great church that taught us that it was God's will that we prosper, but I just did not see that happening, and I had no clue why it wasn't. To be blunt, I really did not see any of my friends prospering to a great degree either.

The Wake-up Call

Everything came to a head when an attorney, one of many who were hounding me for money, called again. This time, he was very to the point and blunt. "Mr. Keesee, I am going to give you three days to send me the $1,600 you owe my client or I will be forced to file a lawsuit against you for that amount." He then simply hung up the phone.

I knew it was over. I was done. There was nowhere to turn that I hadn't already exhausted. There was no money, and there was no food. Our refrigerator looked as bleak as our checking account. I had been hoping for one solid week in business that could have pulled us out, but it never came.

In great despair, I climbed up to my little bedroom in the old farmhouse that we rented for $300 a month. I knew that it was not God's will that we live in such financial bondage, yet we were doing anything but prospering.

As I tearfully threw myself across my bed, I cried out to God. Amazingly, as I cried out, I suddenly heard Him respond. Up out of my spirit, I heard this Scripture:

> *And my God will supply all your needs according to His riches in glory in Christ Jesus.*
>
> —Philippians 4:19 (NASB)

I said out loud, "I know that Scripture, but I do not see that in my life." I then heard the Holy Spirit say:

> "I have nothing to do with the mess you are in. The reason you are in this mess is because you do not know how My Kingdom operates." He went on to tell me that His church was living just like Israel did in Pharaoh's time, as slaves. He said, "I want my people financially free!"

Although I did not really know what He meant by Kingdom, I understood that living in debt was not working, and He was implying there was a better way to live that I had not learned. What that was or how it worked, I did not know, but I knew I had to find out.

The first thing I did was head downstairs and grab Drenda. I told her what God had said to me, and I can remember standing there, holding her hand, and repenting to God and to her for the mess I had gotten us into. We committed right there that although we did not understand what God meant when He said Kingdom, we were going to find out. We also committed not to use debt as a lifestyle any longer but had to admit we did not know how. As we prayed, a peace came over me, and I knew that God was going to show us how to do it His way.

But going back to that word Kingdom, I really had no idea what He was talking about. I knew that I was going to heaven, and I had quite a bit of training in the Bible, but still I did not know what He meant. In fact, the word Kingdom was not a word that I knew much about. The only time I could remember it mentioned in the Bible was in the Lord's Prayer.

> *Your Kingdom come, your will be done, on earth as it is in heaven.*
>
> —Matthew 6:10

I thought at the time that this was referring to the future Kingdom that Jesus would someday set up on the earth, but I had no idea what it was really referring to. But after examining the text, I realized that I was wrong. Jesus was telling us how to pray here, right now. We are to pray God's will into the earth. But what is God's Kingdom?

If you have read my previous books, you can skip ahead to chapter 1 if you want, but I believe a review is always warranted when you are about to take a test. Your test, the game of life, has already begun, but don't worry. There is plenty of time yet to get the correct answers and pass. But if you are reading for the first time, what follows is critical!

A New Way of Living

When God told me that I had never learned how His Kingdom worked, I was confused to say the least. Drenda and I did not have any idea what He meant. We prayed and asked God to teach us what He meant when He said we did not know how His Kingdom worked.

So the first thing I had to learn was what a kingdom was in a natural sense. I think this concept is hard for our Western minds to grasp, as we live in an American mind-set of democracy and free expression. God's Kingdom is not a democracy; it is a kingdom with a king. The authority of the king travels down through the kingdom, with delegated authority, through various government agencies and people who operate under that authority. Having a mob of people is not a kingdom. You could have a million people in a mob, and it would not be a kingdom. A kingdom is a group of people who are held together by law or government.

The definition of kingdom in the dictionary is: "kingdom: a state or government having a king or queen as its head."

Although we celebrate Jesus coming to Earth at Christmas, we usually fail to understand that He was bringing a government with Him. The Bible speaks of this government in Isaiah 9:6-7:

> *For to us a child is born, to us a son is given, and the government will be on his shoulders. And he will be called Wonderful Counselor, Mighty God, Everlasting Father, Prince of Peace. Of the greatness of his government and peace there will be no*

end. He will reign on David's throne and over his kingdom, establishing and upholding it with justice and righteousness from that time on and forever. The zeal of the Lord Almighty will accomplish this.

Jesus is the head of this government, and when we accept Jesus as our personal Savior, we become beneficiaries of that government; we become citizens. Not only do we become citizens, but also we actually become part of God's very own household as sons and daughters.

Yet to all who did receive him, to those who believed in his name, he gave the right to become children of God—children born not of natural descent, nor of human decision or a husband's will, but born of God.

—John 1:12-13

Consequently, you are no longer foreigners and strangers, but fellow citizens with God's people and also members of his household.

—Ephesians 2:19

As members of God's household, we become part of his family and thus own or are part of everything He owns. Also, we become citizens of His great Kingdom with legal rights and benefits.

A New Kingdom

To get a better understanding of what I am talking about, let me talk about being a natural citizen of the United States. As a citizen of the United States, you have legal rights. Your legal rights are written in our Constitution and in the laws that have been passed within our government. These laws and benefits are passed down to every citizen, no matter who they are. Those rights are not based on our feelings or intelligence. No, they are established by law and are legally available to every citizen who calls America their home. It is possible that a citizen may not even know their legal rights, but nevertheless, they have them simply by being a citizen of the United States of America.

Now, here is something to think about, and I hope it changes your entire view of God and how you receive from God. Here in the United States, if we know that something or someone is trying to take our legal rights away from us or that we have been treated unjustly, we have access to justice (justice means enforcement or administration of law), a process which enforces our legal rights. We go to court, and the judge pays no attention to our looks, or how rich or poor we are. He looks at the law. He is to rule in favor of the law every time. The law and the judge are there as our securities.

We have legal rights, and our government will guarantee and enforce our legal rights through a process of justice within the United States' legal system. With that in mind, take a closer look at Isaiah 9 as it talks about this new government that Jesus brought to Earth.

> *He (Jesus) will reign on David's throne and over his kingdom, establishing and upholding it with justice and righteousness....*
> —Isaiah 9:7

This Scripture says that God's Kingdom is established and upheld through justice, the administration of God's law. Administration means the process of implementing or enforcing your legal rights.

Your legal rights are what God calls righteousness or what He says is right, His law. To ensure that you have what God says is right within His Kingdom, what is legally yours as a citizen in that Kingdom, God has given you access to justice, the process or guarantee that you will have what He has promised you.

God has made His will known to us by His Word, the Bible, so we would know our legal rights in His Kingdom. This is good news! Everything you read in the Bible pertaining to what God has promised you is already legally yours as a citizen of His Kingdom!

Second Corinthians 1:20 clearly states that every promise— EVERY PROMISE—is "Yes" and "Amen." It has already been decided; they are already legally yours.

> *For no matter how many promises God has made, they are "Yes"*
> *in Christ. And so through him the "Amen" is spoken by us to the*
> *glory of God.*
>
> —2 Corinthians 1:20

The very foundation of God's Kingdom is justice and righteousness—it can't waver. So think of it this way: if I know the law of God's Kingdom (His will), and I know that I have access to justice, the process of enforcement that guarantees me what the law says, then I am confident and not afraid.

> *This is the confidence we have in approaching God: that if we*
> *ask anything according to his will, he hears us. And if we know*
> *that he hears us—whatever we ask—we know that we have*
> *what we asked of him.*
>
> —1 John 5:14-15

When this verse says He hears us, it is not talking about hearing us audibly as in hearing our words through sound waves; it is talking about Him taking the case.

Think of a judge who hears a case to ensure that justice is done. The courtroom and the judge are there to insure that justice is available to every citizen. The judge's decision is not based on his feelings but based on the law, which he presides over to enforce for every citizen. The judge is there to ensure that justice (the enforcement of law) has taken place according to the written law.

In God's case, His throne (place of authority) and His power are there to ensure justice (the enforcement of His will) to all men who come to Jesus and His Kingdom.

Please read that statement again very slowly, and let it bounce off of your current view of God. Most people feel that God makes His decisions on a case-by-case basis, but that is not true. He is the King of a Kingdom with laws that do not change. He does not and will not make decisions outside of His law. We can know what His answer is before we ask, and we can be certain that we have what His law says before we see it because He has the power to carry out the enforcement of His law.

No More Begging

As Drenda and I began to learn of our legal rights in the Kingdom, it dramatically changed how we thought about God and the Bible. The result of our new understanding changed how we lived. No more begging. No more pleading. We learned what legally already has been given to us as citizens of His Kingdom. And we continued to learn how to lay claim to those promises and see them released here in the earth realm. It was quite a revelation to learn that we are owners of all that heaven has. As citizens, we have legal access to the laws of the Kingdom. But as members of the household itself, we are owners and have a legal claim on the inheritance of all that heaven has.

> *Now if we are children, then we are heirs—heirs of God and* **co-heirs** *with Christ.*
>
> —Romans 8:17

Notice the text says we are co-heirs with Christ! That means everything that Christ has is also ours!

When God spoke to me in my little broken-down farmhouse that day and told me that I did not know how His Kingdom operated, He was referring to the laws and legal structure of His Kingdom. He was right. I had no idea what a kingdom was or how it worked. But one thing I quickly grabbed ahold of, which helped my understanding of a kingdom, was that kingdoms operate by unchangeable laws. Laws show no favoritism. They do not change to favor a certain person. No, they are immovable and constant.

Let me give you an example. Today we enjoy electricity and the light it provides in our homes. You would agree that the laws that govern electricity have always been here since the earth was created. Yet, for thousands of years, there were no lights! The reason? No one had discovered the laws that governed electricity and how to use them to light a light bulb. Although lightning and static electricity were observed as a normal part of life, that is all they were, observations. No one actually thought of duplicating what they were seeing because they did not realize that what they saw was based on natural law that could be learned.

This same lack of understanding permeates the church today.

People read about the great things God did in the Bible but never get past an observational understanding of what they are reading.

Many have seen God do some pretty amazing things in their lives, but like watching a brilliant flash of lightning in a summer storm, they stand there and say, "Wow, did you see that?" yet cannot duplicate it because they do not understand the laws that govern what they just saw. For instance, today, we can place lights anywhere in the world, wherever we want, because we understand the laws that govern electricity.

In the same way, today we also enjoy the ability to travel thousands of miles in a day by jet anywhere in the world. The airplane gains its ability to fly by our understanding and utilizing the law of lift. However, that law has been in the earth since the earth was created, as evidenced by the birds that use that law every day. But no one flew airplanes for thousands of years of human existence because no one had discovered the law of lift and learned how to use it.

Again, it is the same with the Kingdom of God. Most people beg, cry, and carry on trying to convince God to do something on their behalves. But what they do not know is that when they became believers, all the laws and benefits of the Kingdom became theirs to use and enjoy, no begging required.

Let's say I was coming to your church. Would have the prayer team pray and fast that the lights would be on the night I got there? Of course not! If, by chance, I arrived at your church and the lights were not on, would everyone begin to cry out to God, begging and crying trying to convince God to turn the lights on? No, they would look for the switch, simply give it a flip upwards, and the lights would come on. No fear, no confusion, simply turn them on!

But for some reason, Christians have never approached the Kingdom and the Word of God from this perspective. Again, they spend most of their time begging, hoping something will happen. When it does not happen, they immediately blame God, believing that God has chosen not to grant their request. This lack of understanding is why the majority of Christians today believe that God allows bad things to happen, or that He knows best when a tragedy occurs. Friend, this is NOT how the Kingdom of God operates!!!! Again, let's look at our Scripture in 1 John.

> *This is the confidence we have in approaching God: that if we ask anything according to his will, he hears us. And if we know that he hears us—whatever we ask—we know that we have what we asked of him.*
>
> —1 John 5:14-15

Since we know we are asking according to our legal right, and that He takes the case, we are confident that we have what we have asked of Him! Sadly, the truth that is revealed in this text is not understood by a large majority of believers. In my experience, I would have to say by most. But it was this understanding that literally changed my life!

Vision Versus Survival

I began to read the stories in the Bible with renewed interest. I knew that in each story there were spiritual laws to be discovered. I became a spiritual scientist. In every story, I would ask questions. "Why did that happen?" "What law is illustrated in this story?" Slowly, I began to learn the principles and laws that are mine in the Kingdom of God, and it literally changed my life.

As we began to apply these laws, we became completely debt free in two and a half years. We began to pay cash for our cars, built our dream home on 55 acres, and so much more. The best part is now there is no financial pressure. Our home is paid for, and we can now focus on our assignment, our purpose, instead of survival.

We were so excited about what we were learning and yet not seeing most of our friends and acquaintances enjoying the same things we saw happening. Out of our desire to help people learn what we had learned, we launched Faith Life Church in 1995. We focused on sharing the laws and principles that God had taught us, sharing with people how they could be free and live the good life of the Kingdom.

Then in 2005, we launched Faith Life Now, which is our media ministry. Faith Life Now broadcasts our two daily television shows— *Fixing the Money Thing* and *Drenda*—to every time zone in the world with the Good News of the Kingdom.

Today, we are not looking for quarters and dimes buried in our car seats hoping to find enough change to buy a Happy Meal to split between three kids. We spend millions to do what we do now, and we have a passion to help people learn how we did that.

We suddenly moved from survival thinking to vision based thinking and started dreaming of what we could create and do with our lives. We went from financial chaos and slavery to financial freedom.

In our broke and enslaved days, every small cash flow issue was a major emergency. Under great stress, we would try to find someone to borrow the money from, or we would visit our local pawn shop again! But today, we are enjoying the Power of Provision.

You may ask, "Gary, what is the Power of Provision?" The power of provision is the ability to find your purpose and escape a lifetime of survival. Always remember that provision is pro-vision. Read that again slowly; it is a kind of play on words, but the meaning is apparent.

Having no provision leaves behind a life of slavery, and slaves do not dream big dreams! And always remember, you are not a slave! You are a member of God's very household, an heir with Jesus of the entire estate. So lift up your eyes and see a new future. I want you free to dream, free to have fun creating your vision, and living the good life. I trust as we go through this book you will be inspired, but not only inspired, that you will become confident. The same laws of the Kingdom that changed my life are yours as well.

—Gary Keesee

This is actually the fourth book in a five-book series entitled, "Your Financial Revolution." I would encourage you to read the previous three books to gain a good understanding of the laws that I am referencing and more about how the Kingdom of God operates. They are: *Your Financial Revolution: The Power of Allegiance, Your Financial Revolution: The Power of Rest*, and *Your Financial Revolution: The Power of Strategy*. You can find them at GaryKeesee.com or at Amazon.com.

CHAPTER 1
LIGHT SHINES IN THE DARKNESS

I told you in the introduction about the attorney's call which caused me to come face-to-face with the reality of our situation and to finally cry out to God. I also told you what the Lord spoke to me as I lay across my bed weeping, that I was in the mess I was in because I had never learned how His Kingdom operated. But how does it work? What was He trying to show me? I had no clue, but I was about to learn.

If you remember, I had to have that $1,600 dollars to the attorney in three days to avoid a lawsuit. At the time, we had no money and no prospect of having the money from our business in time to pay the $1,600. I was in an impossible situation, or so I thought. Instead, I was about to learn my first lesson with the Kingdom.

At the time, I was driving an old Dodge Caravan which smoked like a chimney when it went down the road. That night, I had an appointment with a family to discuss their insurance needs, and our appointment was at their home, which was about a 15-minute drive from my office.

In those days, I would intentionally park down the street or around the corner from my client's home. The reason was simple. Whenever I started up the van, it always filled the air with white smoke, and I did not think it promoted my business well since I was a so-called financial expert advising my clients how to invest and buy insurance.

Well, on this particular night, like always, I parked just around the corner from my client's home. We had a great visit, and I said good-bye but was concerned when the gentleman proceeded to walk with me as I headed toward my car. Although a bit unnerving, I was fine with that as long as he did not stay around to watch it start, which sadly, he did. Although I took my time in organizing my briefcase and other items in the van trying to give him time to leave, he patiently stood there until I figured I had to go ahead and start it up. Well, as expected, the street filled with white smoke.

As I was about to put the van in drive, he motioned to me to turn it off and came over to the window. He then told me that he worked on cars part-time to make extra money, and he would like to look under the hood. I said sure and popped the hood for him. I knew it didn't really matter what he found. I did not have any money at the moment to put into that old van.

In a few minutes, he came back and said, "Just as I suspected, you have a busted head gasket. Drive it home, and get it fixed before you drive any further. It should only cost you about $700."

I thanked him for his advice and left to head back to my office. All I could hear in my head was, "All it should cost you is about $700!" To me at that moment, $700 sounded like a million dollars, and I still needed to find that $1,600 to send to the attorney. Besides that, I had a pile of other bills that needed paid.

I had no answer, but I remembered the prayer that Drenda and I had prayed earlier, "God, teach us how your Kingdom operates, and show us how to live debt free."

Driving back to the office, I began to talk to the Lord about my financial situation. "Lord, you know all about the money I need. You know I still owe money on this van, and now the $700 is needed. Lord, quite frankly, counting the money I owe the bank for the van and the cost of the repair, it would probably be better if it just burned up and the insurance check paid it all off!" I said that out loud in a frustrated, sarcastic way, not really in an actual prayer.

The minute I said that, something caught my attention. I was not sure if it had always been there, but it seemed that there was a small bubble on the top of the front hood. As I gazed at it, it seemed to be slowly getting bigger. And as I continued to watch the bubble, I was convinced that it was indeed growing in size. I was shocked, to say the least. I did not see any smoke other than the smoke that always seemed to trail behind the van, so I continued on to the office.

As I pulled into the office parking lot, the front of the van suddenly burst into a ball of fire! Flames were gushing out of the engine compartment six feet into the air. I then actually said these words out loud, "Lord, you heard me say that?"

The next day, the insurance company covered the claim, and I had enough money to overnight the $1,600 I owed the attorney as well as pay off the van and still have enough cash left over to buy some groceries. We were happy and shocked all at the same time but without a van, which we needed for all six of us to get around.

I THEN ACTUALLY SAID THESE WORDS OUT LOUD, "LORD, YOU HEARD ME SAY THAT?"

I really could not explain what happened at the time, but the fact that I had said out loud for the van to burn up caught my attention. I had to admit that I had never had any vehicle I owned ever catch on fire before. On the other hand, I had never spoken out loud that I wanted one to either.

Was this tied to the Kingdom? Did I do something to cause this to happen, or was it just a coincidence? We were not sure. Although we celebrated the victory of paying off the van and the creditor, we still needed a van, but how?

Finding a New Van

My dad called to see how we were doing and to offer some help in replacing the burned van. My dad had money, and I was secretly hoping that he would just buy us one. He suggested that we go look at a few dealerships in the area for a good used vehicle. Of course, I wholeheartedly accepted the offer.

We went to a couple of dealerships, and I found the perfect Dodge Caravan. It was about a year old and in mint condition. I told my dad that I thought this one is what Drenda would like, a burgundy beauty, hoping he would say something like, "Great! Well, let's go write it up." But that is not what he said. Instead, he said, "I will give you $5,000 toward the purchase." Yes, that was a very generous offer, but he was really offering to cover the down payment, leaving me to finance the rest.

I was suddenly shocked into reality. I did not have a credit rating that would entice any bank to loan me the money. And up until this moment, I had been able to hide our dire financial condition from my father. Secondly, I felt that I just could not take on more debt.

However, with no other option that I knew of, I made a quick decision to at least fill out the credit application. However, I knew to do that, I would have to confess my situation to my dad and he would have to cosign. I reluctantly told my dad the whole story, he offered to cosign the loan, and we submitted it. The dealership told me they would let me know in the morning.

Of course, I knew that the bank would approve the loan as my dad had perfect credit. Being approved for the loan wasn't what was bothering me as I drove home. I knew I couldn't take that loan, but I had a real need and no money. What was I to do? I was confused and a little distraught.

When I got home and told Drenda the situation, she also knew we could not sign another debt paper, but what other option did we have? We both had a hard time sleeping that night, but in the morning, we were convinced that borrowing the money was not what we should do.

So I called my dad and thanked him for the offer, telling him we just could not take on more debt to finance the car. I then called the dealership and let them know we would not be coming by. They told me, of course, that the van loan had been approved and the van was clean and ready for delivery. I thanked them but insisted I just could not take the van.

As I hung up, I had peace, but at the same time, I had no idea how we would be able to purchase a vehicle big enough for our entire family of six to fit in. I did have a used five-seat coupe that I drove for business that we would have to make do with until we thought of something. About two weeks went by, and we made do with our five-seat coupe, making multiple trips when we needed to get somewhere.

Then one day, I received a phone call from a gentleman that Drenda had bumped into a couple of months before. She had been looking for a few items to sell in her parents' antique auction they held every month in Atlanta, where they lived. They would come to Ohio once a month to buy for their auction, and Drenda would keep her eyes open for anything she thought would be of interest to her parents. It brought in a little extra money each month as they would give her a commission on whatever she found.

As it turned out, Drenda had run into this guy somewhere, and they had gotten into a conversation about what she did and what he did. She mentioned to him that if he ever had anything to sell, she might be interested. Apparently, he ran a fairly large nursing home, and every once in a while, a patient would need to liquidate their belongings when they moved into the home. When there was no family to take care of the household items they needed to get rid of, he would store them in some extra space he had and eventually sell them.

I did not know him, so when he called, I made a note and told Drenda he had called. To make a long story short, when she called him back, he told her that he had three rooms of furniture and household items that he needed to clear out and asked if she would be interested. He offered all of it as a take-all for a very low price.

Drenda and I went to look at the rooms, and although we could not get through the rooms to see everything, as the rooms were packed floor to ceiling, we saw a few things that we felt, if sold, should cover the price he was asking for the lot. We called her parents, and they wired us the money, brought their truck up, and took everything back to Atlanta for their monthly auction.

The auction was a huge success, and for our commission, they agreed to give us a Peugeot station wagon that was just a few years old and in excellent condition. Now I know to most people, getting a used car may not be a reason for a great celebration. But to us, at the time, this was the first time we were driving a car with no payment on it. The car had just been repainted and looked brand new. We were thrilled.

All of a sudden, I was beginning to see it. I could trust God to help me with what I needed without debt.

A Paradigm Shift

Another event that I had with the Lord a year earlier, while we still lived in Oklahoma, now became clearer to me. Looking back, I could see the Lord was trying to get my attention, but we were so far in debt and pressure that for some reason, we just were not seeing what God was trying to teach us.

I love to hunt, and especially I love to hunt deer. But I also like to eat venison and have something to show for my hunting efforts. As it was, I was hunting but had nothing to show for all the effort for the past few years. I would go out, sit in the cold, and go day after day without even seeing a deer. This got a little discouraging as I had babies to feed and sure could have used the venison. Although I had some success in the past, it had been years since I had a successful deer season and brought home the meat.

One day, as I was thinking about the upcoming deer season, I heard the Lord's voice. He said, "Why don't you let Me show you how to get your deer this year?" That startled me. "Show me how to get my deer?" What does that mean?

Praying about those words, I felt the Holy Spirit impress upon me to sow a financial seed or gift for the exact purpose of harvesting that deer. I had never sowed money expecting to harvest a deer before, and it felt a little strange at first. But I clearly felt the Lord leading me to sow that seed with some very detailed instructions while doing so. I was to write out a check for the amount that I felt led to sow. I was to have Drenda and I both lay our hands on it and declare we had received my 1987 buck then and there, when we prayed, not later when I would harvest it, but when we prayed.

Although as a Christian, I had always given and supported my church, sowing like this with a focused intent and believing that I receive when I pray was new to me.

So I took a check and wrote in the memo section, "For my 1987 deer." I laid my hands on it with Drenda, mailed it to a ministry that I had confidence in, and declared that I had just received my deer as I mailed it. I took a piece of paper and wrote on it the day and the time that I believed that I had received the deer and put it in my hunting coat pocket.

Living in the Tulsa, Oklahoma, city limits at the time, I really did not have a place to hunt, but a friend of mine from church invited me to come down to his grandma's home in the country for Thanksgiving; and he said there were a few deer around the farm.

So my family headed down Thanksgiving morning to enjoy a great day of food and fellowship and now to bag my deer. My friend did not really know where to tell me to go, but there was a pasture that was bordered by woods on the property, and he suggested that I go out to the pasture and sit next to a big tree that was there.

Now, I want you to get this picture. As the sun slowly lit my surroundings, I saw that I was sitting in the middle of a mowed hayfield that had one big tree in the middle of it. I felt I was totally in the wrong place as I knew that no self-respecting deer was going to show himself with me sitting right out in the open in that hayfield.

I was just about to get up and move toward the woods, which were about 130 yards in front of me, when I heard movement in the woods along the fencerow off to my left. I could hear leaves rustling off in the distance, and I knew it was deer.

Suddenly, three does came into view walking inside the woods along the fence. I only had a quick glimpse of them as they made their way through the brush. The deer were too far away, but it made me stop and wait a few minutes before I made my move into the woods where I felt the deer would be moving. Then without me knowing it, a buck apparently was running across the field behind me straight for my tree.

I was on the opposite side of the tree as the buck made his way across the field toward the woods in front of me, and he did not see me. The buck ran to the tree, caught my scent, and stopped with a loud snort, which startled me. As I looked to my right at the sudden sound, I was shocked to see a six-point buck staring at me from only about five yards away. Instantly, the buck, now realizing what was going on, took off at a full run toward the woods with high leaping strides.

Now, trying to line up on a whitetail buck that is running full speed with a scoped-out rifle is not an easy target, and I knew that I would only get one shot before he made it to the woods. There was no way I would be able to take careful aim as the deer was jumping with large strides. With only 20 yards to go before the deer would be at the woods, I pulled the trigger. At the shot, the buck fell and did not move. I was shocked! Did this really happen? It all happened so fast! I got up slowly and walked to where the buck lay. I quickly took the note out of my pocket and began to thank God for the deer.

Hearing the sound of the rifle, my friend came out and congratulated me on my buck as he saw it lying there. I had not told my friend about what the Lord had told me, but I looked at him and said, "I don't think this deer was due to my great hunting ability." I then showed him the piece of paper I had written the day Drenda and I prayed for that deer. It simply said, "I believe that I received my 1987 deer on this date and time when I prayed in the name of Jesus." I held up the paper for my friend to see and then began telling him about what the Lord told me to do.

This event caught my attention. I knew without a doubt that it was of God. But for some reason, I had not connected the dots yet.

> **THIS EVENT CAUGHT MY ATTENTION. I KNEW WITHOUT A DOUBT THAT IT WAS OF GOD.**

The concept of Kingdom law and what had happened with the deer affecting my finances had not occurred to me yet. Getting that deer was amazing, but would it happen again? Without the concept of Kingdom law, I would not know how or what laws caused the deer to show up. But I looked forward to testing it again next deer season.

Faith Works Every Time

The next deer season brought change as we moved to Ohio from Tulsa. This move was prompted one day while out jogging. The Holy

Spirit spoke to me and said that it was time to move home to Ohio, and there I would do my end-time work.

I had lived in Tulsa at that point for ten years, and I loved Tulsa, but I could not have been happier at the prospect of leaving. An oil recession that had hit a year earlier hit Tulsa exceptionally hard as its economy was primarily oil based. Our finances had become critical, and we found ourselves barely making ends meet. A fresh start was something I could get excited about. Little did I know that the next nine years would bring even more financial stress that would far surpass what we saw in Tulsa.

We moved to Ohio in early summer, and I looked forward to what Ohio had for us. We found out very quickly that starting our business over again and carrying all of our debt with us to Ohio was extremely stressful.

Of course, deer season was coming up as well as the birth of our third child, Tom. Tom was born on the second day of the Ohio deer season, so obviously, I had no time to scout with the baby coming and starting the business over again. I knew of only one place to hunt.

Across the street from the home I grew up in, I had run a trapline while in high school. My parents' property had a pond on it, which was fed by a small stream that ran across the neighbor's farm and then to our pond. I will have to admit that although I walked that stream for years growing up, I never saw a deer or even saw one deer print on that land. But I remember while in college getting a call from my brother who told me that he was shocked to see a deer back there one day and how he planned to hunt there that coming fall. We were both surprised. I made a mental note of the conversation, which at that point was nine or ten years earlier.

I remembered the exact spot he said he saw the deer, as I was very familiar with the stream. He indicated that he had seen the deer where the stream split and a very large maple tree stood. He then told me that there was a smaller maple tree next to the larger one, and he found that he could use the smaller tree to climb up into the larger tree, which he thought would make a great place to hunt deer from.

Well, my brother never shot a deer back at that stream, although he said he missed one once. But he had not been back there for years either, so I had no idea if the tree was still there or if I could even find it in the dark on the morning of my planned hunt.

To make matters a little trickier, Ohio had a shotgun only law. No rifles were allowed during deer season, only deer slugs from a shotgun. I only had a double barreled 20-gauge at the time and had no confidence I could hit a deer with it except within 20 yards. But that was all I had at the time, so that was my plan.

Drenda and I sowed our seed, laid our hands on the check the same way we did the previous year, and claimed I had my deer according to Mark 11:24. To make a long story short, on the fourth day of Ohio's gun season, my first day out, I harvested a doe and a buck in 40 minutes, both from 75-yard shots that were way beyond my ability with a smooth bore shotgun. Ohio had a two-deer limit at the time, which is why I harvested two deer that year. That's right, I had my two deer in 40 minutes.

Again, I knew I was on to something. But at the time of this deer harvest, our finances were in really bad shape, and the stress was suffocating. It actually never occurred to me to apply this same principle to our finances.

Too Many "Coincidences"

That first winter and the next 12 months in Ohio were horrible as

I battled extreme emotional problems, panic attacks, and depression, as I shared in the introduction of this book.

It was that next November, right before deer season, that the van burned up. Although I had seen the amazing deer harvest for the previous two deer seasons, I still did not have a revelation of the Kingdom. With the van burning up and God speaking to me about the Kingdom, I realized that there

QUITE FRANKLY, GOD WILL USE ANYTHING TO GET YOUR ATTENTION.

was more to these three stories than I had first thought. I felt very encouraged, but even at that point, I had no concept of Kingdom law.

The next deer season came, and I had my deer in about 40 minutes again, just like clockwork. We began to see the Kingdom working in our finances also, which I will cover in chapter 2. But throughout those early years, I would see some amazing things.

Of course, God always seemed to teach me something new when it came to my deer hunting. I think the reason why is because deer season is all about harvest, and it occurs in a controlled and very limited amount of time. The gun season in Ohio is usually open for only two weeks. With such a focused harvest season, you are not wanting to waste time. Instead, most deer hunters are very focused and intent heading into the season. Most will spend hours scouting and preparing for that two-week opportunity. So this makes for a great laboratory to study the Kingdom.

So excuse all the deer hunting stories, but they were very significant to me. They revealed hidden laws that I would not have seen otherwise. Quite frankly, God will use anything to get your attention. He used fishing to catch Peter, James, and John's attention in Luke chapter five when they caught so many fish that their boats about sank. It just so happened that in my case He used deer hunting.

After God spoke to me about the Kingdom in my bedroom that day, and after I saw the van burn and remembered the deer hunts, and then how God opened a door for us to earn that great used station wagon with no debt, suddenly, we were getting it. Drenda and I were all in.

I started studying the Bible in a whole new way. I called myself a spiritual scientist. I began to ask questions. "Why did that happen? Why didn't that happen?" I was looking closely for clues of the spiritual laws behind the stories I was reading in the Bible.

God kept showing me things; and again, He used deer hunting to show me more of the Kingdom. This next story really caught my attention. It was another one of those "Did you see that?" moments.

It was Halloween evening, and I had about 45 minutes until our family was to head to the church to attend a party we were holding as an alternative to the traditional demon inspired celebration.

Drenda and I had sowed our seed for a buck, laid our hands on the check, sent it to a ministry that we believed God showed us, and called it done according to Mark 11:24 a couple of weeks earlier. This would be my first time out for the season, and I was bowhunting on the land that we rented.

Even though I was pressed for time, since God told me how to hunt by faith, I would usually get my deer within 40 minutes, so I felt it would be close but I had time to get my buck. On this particular day, I went to my tree stand on the back of the pinewoods that were behind our old farmhouse and climbed up. I was not there for more than 10 minutes when I spotted the buck about 200 yards away from me heading into my neighbor's woods. I knew that he was my buck, but he was heading the wrong way!

This was only the second year I was bowhunting, and I really did not know that much about it. I was not wearing camouflage, did not own a grunt call, and had not even heard of using scents to attract deer. My tree stand was a board that I had nailed between two limbs only about 12 feet off the ground, which if you know anything about bowhunting from a tree stand, is really not high enough. But the year before, my first year bowhunting, I harvested two deer for the two times I had gone out using my faith, and I did not expect anything different this year.

As I watched the buck heading in the wrong direction, I did not know what to do, so I began to pray. All of a sudden, I heard the Holy Spirit speak to me. He said, "Tell the buck to come to you." I was a little shocked by that. Tell the deer to come to me? I knew I could not yell out loudly, so I just said in a conversational voice, "Deer, stop! Turn around, and come and stand under my tree." Crazy, right? No grunt call, nothing. But the second I said that, the buck stopped, looked both directions, then turned around and began to walk the 200 yards toward me. Even though the woods I was in were about 400 yards wide, that buck walked straight to my tree, walked directly under it, and stood still.

Of course, I could not miss that shot. Wow! Did I just see that? The deer fell below me with a clean shot. I glanced at my watch and realized that if I was going to make it to the party, I had better leave the deer there until I could return and take it up to the barn. I will have to admit I thought about what I saw for weeks after that. But God was not finished getting my attention.

The farm we rented had a creek running through it with a lot of brush along it. There was always some good rabbit hunting. This particular day, it had snowed during the night, and snow always made it easier to see the rabbits. I could not resist, so my son Tim and I were working our way down the creek bottom, kicking brush piles as we went, when all of a sudden, a cock pheasant flew out of the brush.

Ohio did have a pheasant season, but I hardly ever saw a pheasant on the farm, maybe one a year. Well, as this one took off, I was thrilled to have a shot at one. As I took the shot, the bird fell but hit the ground running. I instantly knew what I had done. I had nicked its wing. The bird was running at full strength up the hill from the creek, and a cock pheasant can run up to 35 miles an hour. Of course, with the snow, he was not going that fast, but he was going fast.

Since the creek was in the bottom of a long ravine, I had a full view of every square inch of the hillside. The hill had been used to grow sod the previous year, so it was very flat with only an occasional tuft of grass sticking up.

As the bird was going at a full run up the hill, I knew there was no way I could catch it, and it was out of range for the shotgun. But all of a sudden, I remembered the buck, how it came to me when I spoke. So I yelled out loud, "Pheasant, STOP!" At the instant I said that, the pheasant disappeared. I had a clear, open view of the entire hillside, which was covered in snow with only an occasional tuft of grass sticking out above the snow, yet he was gone. Tim yelled, "Where did it go, Dad?" "I don't know," I replied.

So we began to follow its tracks up the hill, and there it was just sitting there with its little head tucked under the snow. I thought, "Well, did I hit it and it ran until it died?" I reached down and grabbed the bird, and it burst into a squawking, wings flapping, wild pheasant. It was very much alive! That night when I butchered the bird, I looked it over very closely. There were not any pellet marks on the bird, but I saw where I had indeed nicked the right wing. So the bird was indeed very alive but had stopped the very second I yelled, "Stop!"

Yes, Lord, you have my full attention!

CHAPTER 2
A NEW WAY OF THINKING

As Drenda and I began to see the Kingdom operate in our lives, we just could not stop telling people about it. We knew that we were on an exciting road of discovery and deliverance. I was still selling insurance and securities, but I felt something was changing. I did not know what, but I knew that there had to be answers for my finances just as I had seen in my deer hunting and as I had seen in obtaining that great used station wagon. I knew I needed more than just owning a great used station wagon, although I was certainly excited to have it.

I still had a lot of debt at this point in our story. I wanted to be free of debt but had no idea what to change. Even though I did not know what to change, I was sure I was going to find out. I knew that I had discovered my answer, but again, I needed to learn more about how to get the pictures I saw in the Bible to actually manifest in my life. My business, as it stood at the time, was barely covering our living expenses. But that was better than it had been when we were falling further into debt each month.

Drenda and I kept reading the Bible and searching for more clues regarding the Kingdom's function. We sowed our money for the finances we needed as well.

Then one night, I had a dream. In the dream, I saw a caterpillar slowly crawling up the stalk of a plant. It then crawled out on a stem and wove a cocoon. Suddenly, out of the cocoon came a beautiful butterfly, which then flew away. A voice then said, "So shall your business be."

I woke up and understood what the dream meant. A caterpillar can only crawl and is very limited in how it lives it life, usually living on the same plant its entire life. But a transformation takes place that changes the potential and the entire life of that caterpillar. It transforms itself into a butterfly, which allows it to fly anywhere it wants to go. Some, like the Monarch, can fly thousands of miles to avoid the winter months in the northern hemisphere. Although at the time of the dream I did not know how this transformation was going to take place, I knew that God was showing me that it was going to take place. I was encouraged.

An Amazing Discovery

As was my practice since moving back to Ohio, I would make 90 cold calls a day in the morning. I wish I could tell you I had a great system to do this, but quite frankly, I just went through the phone book each day (this was before the Do Not Call list).

Since I was a regional vice president for the company I worked for, my main function was to hire and train new sales reps. I would call and say that my company was expanding in Ohio, and I was making some calls in the area to see if they knew of anyone that might be interested. Most of the time, I would get an answering machine and would leave a message. If they had an interest, they would call back. By making the 90 calls a day, I could expect to set up two to three interviews and a possible sale.

It was through this process that I met Dave. In talking to him on the phone, he expressed his desire to find a new career field and was interested to see what I had to offer. I offered to come by his home that evening, and he said that would be fine. As I sat down with him and his wife, I began to ask all the normal questions about where he worked now, why he wanted a career change, and where they were at financially. I usually always asked potential candidates about their personal finances because if, in fact, they did not decide they had an interest in the company, I then approached the call as a potential sale. So gathering financial data allowed me to get an idea of how much insurance they should consider and to see what other insurance products they may already have.

To my amazement, while we were discussing their current financial condition, the wife began to cry in despair. Their finances were upside down, and they had no idea what to do or what to change. I realized that their problem was not insurance. They needed to increase their cash flow and get out of debt, so I also mentioned the Kingdom of God and how Drenda and I were learning how it worked. I assured them that I would do all I could do to help them and would meet with them again in a week to discuss any changes that they may need to implement.

On the way to the office after that appointment, I was troubled. There had to be something I could do!

As I made it back to the office, I sat down at my desk and suddenly had an idea. I would research options for any product or service they were using to hopefully find the same service at a lower price. My goal was to see how much money I might be able to free up that they could use for debt reduction. This was in the days before the Internet, so all my searching had to be through the Yellow Pages and phone calls.

After a week, I had price checked every product or service they were using and really was quite amazed at what I had found. By rearranging or replacing their current vendors with vendors or companies that were less expensive, I freed up over $600 a month in cash flow. I then took my financial calculator and applied the freed up cash flow to their current debt structure and hit the calculate button.

As the number showed up on the screen, I sat there stunned. Surely, I had made a mistake somewhere. My calculation showed that this couple could be completely out of debt in less than seven years, including their home mortgage, without changing their income. *Impossible*, I thought. So I worked the numbers again with the same results.

I then went to my file drawer and pulled a few of my other clients' files out and worked through those that week. Just like my current client, every one of them could be completely out of debt in five to seven years, including their mortgage, without changing their current income. If this was possible, and I now knew it was, why wasn't someone shouting this from the rooftops? I typed up a sheet of data for my client that showed them how they could be completely out of debt in less than seven years. I was so excited to meet back up with them and show them what I had discovered, and was curious as to how they would receive that information.

As I sat down with Dave and his wife, I went through the numbers one item at a time explaining how the money could be freed up. I purposely hid the final results until I completely went through every item that could free up cash flow. Throughout my presentation, my clients sat there almost in shock. From their perspective, there was no money and no way to get out of debt—ever! As I flipped the final page over, revealing that they could be free in less than seven years, including their home mortgage, suddenly, the husband jumped up with tears in his eyes. He was so excited. They both now broke down in tears and thanked me over and over again for coming by. I then spent some time sharing with them all that God had been revealing to me and what I had learned so far regarding the Kingdom of God. They were all ears!

I did not make one penny from that client, but I was the happiest I had ever been with a client; and now my mind was spinning a million miles an hour. I wanted to do what I just did for every client I saw, and I asked the Lord for wisdom on how to monetize the process. I knew this was going to be my new business model if I could figure out how to make any money doing it. After some trial and error, we found a way to offer our plans for free to anyone who asked and yet also bring in cash flow for our business through a referral system we designed. It was too good to believe, and Drenda and I were so excited.

I knew this was the transformation that I had seen in the dream. Although I knew we were just at the cocoon stage of the dream, I was so ready to fly! There was much I had to learn yet to really fly, but I knew I was on the right track.

We incorporated our new company and called it Faith-Full Family Finances because we knew that with faith, your finances would stay full; and that was the message we really wanted to convey, even more than the financial answers we offered. We retained that name for over 20 years but realized that the name was obviously a Christian name, and we wanted to reach more unbelievers, so we decided to change our name to Forward Financial Group, which it is today. (By the way, we still do those free debt plans as well as help people avoid market risk for their retirement accounts. You can reach Forward Financial Group at 1-(800)-815-0818 or online at Forwardfinancialgroup. com.)

Although we were still in serious debt at the time of launching our company, we knew we were heading the right way. The company was a huge success, and Drenda and I became debt free in about two and one-half years. I cannot tell you how exciting that was! All of a sudden, our lives were not consumed with survival, and vision began to spring up on the inside of us.

Paying cash for a new car was awesome. Buying and paying cash for 55 acres of some of the most beautiful land in Ohio was beyond words. Building our 7,700 square foot dream home and having it paid for was beyond incredible! I will never forget standing there with Drenda watching the basement to our new home being dug. The basement was bigger than the entire little farmhouse we were living in. We both stood there with tears rolling down our faces watching that. Watching nine years of hell on Earth falling behind us. Knowing that things would never be the same. We discovered the Kingdom of God, and we now knew why it was called good news by the prophet Isaiah.

> *The Spirit of the Sovereign Lord is on me, because the Lord has anointed me to proclaim good news to the poor.*
> —Isaiah 61:1

To be honest, Drenda and I had to pinch ourselves over and over again because such incredible things were happening. Being completely out of debt was once an impossible dream, but now it was a reality!

Listen, I am not this good! You saw my track record. I tried it my way for years and worked hard with nothing but heartache and stress. I was learning how to do life God's way, and it was working. And that is why you are reading this book, to find out what I found out, and find out you will. But first you must realize that I had tapped into a new system, a new Kingdom, and a completely new way of doing life. This is your answer as well. This is the answer you need. This is the good news you have been waiting for. I know, I know, your church doesn't teach this stuff. Well, mine did not either, but all of it is right there in the Bible.

God Is Good—Always

So let me give you a major key to understanding what I am saying—dump the religion! This is not a religious issue. It is about God, what He wants you to have, and how He paid the price through Jesus to give you the Kingdom. So, let's dig into the Kingdom and find out how it works.

As Drenda and I began to see the Kingdom of God operate in our lives, many times, we were shocked at what we saw. We realized that the majority of believers had no idea how it worked.

For instance, I just read a headline of a seven-year-old that died on the operating table during a tonsillectomy. Though an extremely common and usually very safe operation, her heart just stopped during the operation, an extremely grievous outcome. I think all of our hearts sighed a bit just hearing that it happened. However, as tragic as the event was, there was another tragic part of the story that could affect this family for the rest of their lives. Let me quote what the father said to a reporter, and I am quoting here.

> "You don't understand why these things happen, but we know it was God's plan. And that's the only thing that can get us through, because we know it was God."[3]

---

3 https://nypost.com/2020/02/26/7-year-old-south-carolina-girl-dies-during-tonsillectomy

Let me also quote Green Bay Packers' quarterback Aaron Rodgers, whose story appeared January 22nd, 2020, in *People* magazine.[4]

> Rodgers explained that he questioned religion as a kid and has since related to a "different type of spirituality" as he's gotten older. "Most people that I knew, church was just … you just had to go." He also said, "I don't know how you can believe in a God who wants to condemn most of the planet to a fiery hell. What type of loving, sensitive, omnipresent, omnipotent being wants to condemn his beautiful creation to a fiery hell at the end of all this?"

Crazy comments! But if this is what they believe about God, you would have to agree, who could trust or desire to serve a God that wanted to take their seven-year-old daughter? No one! And who wants to serve a God who "wants" to condemn most of the planet to hell? No one! But that is what the majority of Christians believe. You have heard it all your life: "God allowed it," "God did it," "It was God's plan," "It was their time to go," and many more statements like that. In fact, I am going to bet that you probably think the same way. So I am going to be blunt. If you really believe that God is like that, that He would willingly kill a child or give someone cancer, then we need to have a serious talk. Let me say it this way:

YOU WILL NEVER BELIEVE SOMEONE YOU DON'T TRUST!

If you have been taught to distrust God, that He kills innocent people, and if you agree that He is the all-powerful Creator of the universe, then we better all just do our best to stay on His good side.

---

4 https://people.com/sports/aaron-rodgers-opens-up-about-religion-to-danica-patrick-i-dont-know-how-you-can-believe-in-a-god

This is what people did in the past in many primitive cultures. They would make all kind of offerings to appease the God of wrath. They would put themselves under all kinds of restrictions, even submitting to various kinds of pain, to show they were truly submitted to Him and, hopefully, avoid His wrath. But is this really the character of the God of the Bible? Are we to live in fear of God? No, of course not. The concept that God is against us or not trustworthy is all a result of bad teaching that began in the Garden with Adam and Eve.

> *Now the serpent was more crafty than any of the wild animals the Lord God had made. He said to the woman, "<u>Did God really say</u>, 'You must not eat from any tree in the garden'?"*
>
> *The woman said to the serpent, "We may eat fruit from the trees in the garden, but God did say, 'You must not eat fruit from the tree that is in the middle of the garden, and you must not touch it, or you will die.'"*
>
> *"You will not certainly die," the serpent said to the woman. "For God knows that when you eat from it your eyes will be opened, and you will be like God, knowing good and evil."*
>
> *When the woman saw that the fruit of the tree was good for food and pleasing to the eye, and also <u>desirable for gaining wisdom</u>, she took some and ate it.*
>
> —Genesis 3:1-6

Satan has been casting doubts on God's character since time began. Strangely, Eve already had any wisdom she may have felt she was lacking through her relationship with God, Himself. Yet Satan was able to convince her that there was something she was missing that God was withholding from her. Adam and Eve believed a lie about God and willingly cast aside their positions in His Kingdom to pursue a different kingdom. They believed that Satan had a better future for them. Of course, their decision only brought pain, sorrow, and death.

Satan's tactics have never changed, and it is not surprising that his greatest target is the church itself. Because the church already has the authority to put Satan under its feet and defeat him on every front, his only weapons are as they were then, deception and lies.

The Character of God

In regard to your future and your provision, this is the most important topic we need to tackle first, the character of God. If we do not get this issue settled, then you might as well just toss this book aside as just another get rich help book. My hope is that you will give me the time to walk you through this. I hope that you truly want to be financially free and desire wisdom and knowledge. This time, the teaching is not from the liar, Satan, who deceived Adam and Eve, but from God, Himself.

First, I can understand why you feel that God allows bad things to happen. I mean if He is God, then He has the power to do anything, right? So if the seven-year-old dies and God had the power to stop it, then He must have allowed it. Well, that statement is only partly true. Although God had the power to stop it, He did not have the legal jurisdiction to stop it. I will get into this jurisdiction issue in the next chapter, but I need to address the character issue first and then make sure you know, without any wavering or doubt, that God is good and His Word is truth.

You may wonder why this is so important. As we go further in this book, I will be discussing the laws of the Kingdom, their function, and how those laws set me free from the financial hell I was living in. If you do not trust the King, Himself, then His laws will mean nothing to you.

Remember, my first discovery on this journey was that the Kingdom of God is a government. This government has a King who sets the laws of the Kingdom. These laws lay out the available benefits and the responsibilities of the citizens living in the Kingdom. They protect and guarantee to every citizen in the Kingdom the King's will for their lives. To understand the King's character is a prerequisite to understanding the laws themselves.

As I said before, once I understood that the Kingdom of God is a government with laws and benefits that legally belong to every citizen of the Kingdom, I became a spiritual scientist. I then knew that behind every action of the Kingdom, there was a spiritual law that precipitated it. I then had hope. I could learn the laws! Anyone can! This is what Keith and Kathy found out.

Four Years Changed Their Life

Keith and Kathy were just making a paycheck at a normal job, living a normal life. They had just bought a new home when Keith lost his job. However, Keith found out about our *Fixing the Money Thing* TV show a little over a year earlier and had spent time studying and meditating on some of my material, learning about the Kingdom and his legal rights as a citizen.

When he lost his job, he prayed about it and decided that instead of looking for another job, he would start his own trucking company.

He admitted he really did not know much about the business, but he felt he could learn. He started his truck hauling business with one truck and would haul cars and whatever else he could find to haul. As Keith and Kathy kept learning, a new opportunity opened up to start hauling for a national company that needed help. This was a big step for Keith, and it required him to own his own semi and to learn many more laws regarding the trucking transportation business—but he took it and trusted God was leading him.

Since then, the company has just taken off. Now, he has eight semis hauling full-time every day. Keith told me that at his corporate job, he used to make about $1,500 a week. In his first year of owning his own trucking company, Keith said he was making almost $4,000 a week. The second year, Keith jumped to over $15,000 a week. The next year, he jumped to $25,000 a week, and the next year to over $38,000 a week. Keith went from making $78,000 a year to two million a year in four years!

ANYTHING OR ANYONE THAT TELLS YOU THAT GOD IS NOT GOOD IS TELLING YOU A LIE!

I got a text from Keith as I was writing this chapter. He said that he just had to hire four more drivers, and his cash flow is now $70,000 a week. From $78,000 a year to $70,000 a week in a four-year period! That catches my attention! Keith and Kathy are expecting that even greater things are ahead as they are now planning on starting two more companies.

If you asked Keith and Kathy how they did this, they would give all the credit to learning how the Kingdom works.

The first thing that Keith and Kathy would tell you is that they had to unlearn a lot of the religious junk they had been taught all their lives about God and how He works. One of the keys they had to focus on was that God is good, ALWAYS GOOD, and He NEVER lies. Anything or anyone that tells you that God is not good is telling you a lie!

> *Don't be deceived, my dear brothers and sisters. Every good and perfect gift is from above, coming down from the Father of the heavenly lights, who does not change like shifting shadows.*
> —James 1:16-17

Secondly, they would say they had to learn to be givers in a whole new way. Supporting God's assignments with the money that they bring in is an essential key to their success.

The Bible is clear. To blame God for the horrible things that happen to people is not accurate. The Bible says that Satan is the one who comes to kill, steal, and destroy.

> *The thief comes only to steal and kill and destroy; I have come that they may have life, and have it to the full.*
> —John 10:10

And notice what Jesus says after that first statement, "I have come that they may have life and have it to the full," or some versions say life "more abundantly." God is not your enemy. But if you think He is, then according to James 1:16, you have been deceived by someone. You will have to ask yourself who told you that God lies. Who told you that God killed that seven-year-old? Who told you that God sometimes heals and sometimes chooses not to? I can probably guess—some preacher who did not know any better. But here is a statement that you need to hold on to if you are going to receive from God. God does not lie! In fact, the Bible says that it is impossible for Him to lie (Hebrews 6:18).

Again, the reason people believe that God is not always good is because they do not understand the Kingdom's legal system here in the earth realm. As I mentioned earlier, we will dig into that in the next chapter, and it will answer a ton of your questions. But if you want to understand how the Kingdom operates, you must know that God is good and He never lies.

The Constants of God's Kingdom

Way back in high school, I learned a lesson that I think applies here. We were taught that when you are dealing with physical substances, there are certain attributes that never change and are constant. You guessed it! These laws are called constants in physics. For instance, the temperature that causes water to freeze is 32 degrees. That is a constant; it never changes. In the same way, the fact that God is good is a constant. So in regard to water, you would use the constant of water's freezing temperature in all of your equations dealing with water.

The same applies to understanding God's character. If you know that God is good and never changes, you will be able to interpret a passage of Scripture through the lens of that constant. As an example, let's take a look at Exodus 4:11-12 in the King James Version.

And the Lord said unto him, Who hath made man's mouth? or who maketh the dumb, or deaf, or the seeing, or the blind? Have not I the Lord?

—Exodus 4:11-12 (KJV)

At first glance, it looks like God makes people blind and unable to hear on purpose. But we have to remember our constant—that God is always good. Let's take a look at the same Scripture in a different version.

> *Then the Lord asked Moses, "Who makes a person's mouth? Who decides whether people speak or do not speak, hear or do not hear, see or do not see? Is it not I, the Lord?"*
>
> —Exodus 4:11 (NLT)

The context of this passage is that God has called Moses to go to his own people, the Hebrews, and tell them that God has called him to go to Pharaoh to demand that the Hebrews be freed. But Moses says back to God, "What if the Hebrews do not believe that you have appeared to me?" God tells him a few ways to prove it to them. But then Moses pleads with the Lord,

> *"O Lord, I'm not very good with words. I never have been, and I'm not now, even though you have spoken to me. I get tongue-tied, and my words get tangled."*
>
> *Then the Lord asked Moses, "Who makes a person's mouth? Who decides whether people speak or do not speak, hear or do not hear, see or do not see? Is it not I, the Lord? Now go! I will be with you as you speak, and I will instruct you in what to say."*
>
> —Exodus 4:10–12 (NLT)

Let me paraphrase what God was saying to Moses. Did I make man's mouth to speak or not to speak? Did I make man's eyes to see or not to see? The answer is obvious. The mouth was created to speak, and the eyes were created to see. That is all God is trying to get Moses to say. Basically, God is saying, "If I made the mouth, then I certainly can help you use it!" God is trying to get Moses to understand that he can trust Him to help him speak when he goes to the Hebrews.

But without having a correct view of God, we could misinterpret the intent here. I think we have all heard that Moses stuttered. Most people would state that as an absolute fact, but is it? In response, you would say, "Most definitely. Moses, himself said that he did not speak well." I agree, he did say that, but in reference to what? If Moses could not speak well, then we need to explain Acts 7:22.

> *Moses was taught all the wisdom of the Egyptians, and he was powerful in both speech and action.*
> —Acts 7:22 (NLT)

Actually, we see that Moses was just the opposite of someone that had a hard time with words. He was powerful in speech. So what does Moses mean when he says, "O Lord, I'm not very good with words. I never have been, and I'm not now, even though you have spoken to me. I get tongue-tied, and my words get tangled"?

When Exodus 4 is talking about Moses being slow of speech, it is referencing the fact that Moses did not speak the Hebrew language well. He was not raised with the Hebrews. He was raised as an Egyptian and primarily spoke the Egyptian language. God is reassuring Moses that since He made man's mouth, He would help him speak to the Hebrews. But yet again, Moses stalls.

> *But Moses said, "Pardon your servant, Lord. Please send someone else."*

Then the Lord's anger burned against Moses and he said, "What about your brother, Aaron the Levite? I know he can speak well. He is already on his way to meet you, and he will be glad to see you. You shall speak to him and put words in his mouth; I will help both of you speak and will teach you what to do. He will speak to the people for you, and it will be as if he were your mouth and as if you were God to him.

—Exodus 4:13-16

The inference is that Aaron knew the Hebrew language very well, being raised as a Hebrew, and could talk to the Hebrews for Moses, not that Moses stuttered.

So now you see how important having a correct and constant view of God's character is. Knowing that He is always good allows us to question the assumed meaning of the text and to dig deeper for a proper interpretation. So again, your foundation in the Kingdom is to know the character of the King himself. If that is not known, then Satan could deceive you, like he did Eve, into believing that God is not telling all the truth or, worse yet, He has lied to you.

> **THERE ARE OVER 7,000 PROMISES IN THE BIBLE THAT DEFINE YOUR LEGAL RIGHTS AS A CHILD OF GOD.**

Understanding God's Promises

There are over 7,000 promises in the Bible that define your legal rights as a child of God. Each promise is given to you by the King, Himself and can be trusted. Or can it? If doubt can be raised regarding God's goodness, then doubt can be raised regarding His promises as well.

Let me give you an example. Let's say that I gave you a $1,000 check. You would thank me, and in your mind, you would have $1,000. You would act like you have $1,000, talk like you have $1,000, and again thank me for the $1,000. But the fact of the matter is you would not have $1,000; you would have a promissory note. The check is simply a promise that I gave you stating that you have a legal right to receive $1,000 from my bank. You still have to cash the check to actually have the money! But since my intent toward you is known, as I willingly gave you the check and I signed it, and because you trust that I have the $1,000, you would say you have $1,000 when all you really have is a promise.

God is certainly greater than I am. His Word does not lie. He gives us His great and precious promises. If God gives you His promise, it is as good as done! The only thing Satan can do to stop the promise from coming to pass is to make you suspicious of God's Word. This is why it is vital that you know that God is good and does not lie.

Let me give you another example. I know many have heard that miracles have passed away and God does not do the same things that Jesus did as He walked on the earth. I grew up in a very traditional church, and to be honest, I never saw the power of God manifested, at least that I can remember. So just because I did not see people getting healed, does that mean that God does not heal any longer? To answer that, we cannot go by our experience. We need to find out what the Bible says, what the King's law says about healing.

*How God **anointed** Jesus of Nazareth with the Holy Spirit and power, and how he went around doing good and healing all who were under the power of the devil, **because God was with him**.*
—Acts 10:38

As we can see, healing was a key signature of Jesus's ministry.

The text says that Jesus healed all because God was with Him. Now that phrase, "God was with Him" is a statement that you need to understand. Of course, God was with Jesus His entire life on the earth. But this phrase is actually referring to the moment when Jesus was being water baptized and the Holy Spirit descended on Him like a dove. Up until that moment, Jesus had not done any miracles. We have no record of Jesus multiplying His breakfast cereal or healing one person as a child. It was only after He was anointed by the Holy Spirit that His ministry actually began. God was with Him doing the work.

Well, you might say, "Yes, Jesus healed, but He is not here." Well I agree, you are correct, but He passed that assignment on to the church. You see, that same power that came on Jesus was also given to the church. As Jesus is about to leave the earth, He tells His disciples the following.

> *But you will receive power when the Holy Spirit comes on you; and you will be my witnesses in Jerusalem, and in all Judea and Samaria, and to the ends of the earth.*
>
> —Acts 1:8

This same power, the Holy Spirit, came upon the church to do the same miracles that Jesus did.

You cannot tell me anything different. My own daughter Amy had a 13-pound tumor in her abdomen. We all prayed for her healing based on God's Word, and she went to bed then woke up in the morning completely healed. The 13-pound tumor was gone, and her back (which was knotted and twisted) was completely reconstructed. You can see and read her story in her book *Healed Overnight*.

My daughter-in-law had a tumor the size of an orange on her

side, which the doctors said would have to be removed with surgery. They said she had a rare form of cancer and had one to two months to live. She also believed the promises of God and woke up in the morning completely healed. The tumor was gone.

My wife, Drenda, also had a huge growth the size of a 50-cent piece on her back. She began to command it to leave her body, and within two weeks, it was completely gone as well.

Did God choose to heal these ladies? Was it something that God had to make a choice to do? Did He like these three ladies better than you? No! They understood the laws and benefits of the Kingdom and simply laid claim to them. "Well then, why," you might ask, "are so many people sick? Why do we not see people healed more often in our churches?"

I am glad you asked. Let's dig into that in the next chapter.

CHAPTER 3
THE JURISDICTION ISSUE

As I stated earlier, I live out in the country with 60 acres of some of the prettiest land in Ohio. I originally had 55 acres, but my neighbor sold me a piece of land that bordered my land, which brought my total up to 60 acres. We have surely enjoyed this land over the last 22 years. Having woods to hunt deer, a marsh to hunt ducks, and fields to hunt rabbits and pheasants in, as well as run around on our four wheelers in is a blessing. But if you took a close look at my place, you would find on the perimeter of the property NO TRESPASSING signs. The signs are there so people will know where my property line begins.

The law in Ohio says that a person who wants to be on my land must have a written consent form on them at all times when they are on the property. If they do not, it is called trespassing, and they can legally be thrown off and could incur penalties and fines in the process. The issue is that anyone who chooses to walk my land without me knowing it does not have the legal jurisdiction to make that decision, as it is not their land. If I tell them to get off my land, it is not their choice!

So in brief, you cannot occupy something you do not have legal jurisdiction over.

This trespassing illustration will answer so many questions

that people have regarding why things happen or don't happen in the Kingdom of God. Understanding the jurisdiction issue in the Kingdom is a prerequisite to operating with effectiveness in the Kingdom.

Why Weren't They Healed?

I am sure you have probably heard a story like this. Someone gets sick who is well-known, and prayer is called for them. Millions of people join in prayer on behalf of this person's healing, and yet this person dies. Why? Or someone tells you that their grandmother died even though they were praying for her, and they want to know why. Or someone tells you that they have sown money for a financial need, and yet they continue to be broke. Are there answers for these types of questions?

Before I answer that, let's acknowledge that we do not know everything going on in the Spirit realm, and I am not pretending that I do. However, based on the Word of God, we know that if someone is sick, Jesus paid the price for their healing. We know that if we are generous and give, the Bible says we shall receive. Yet on a daily basis, we see what looks like apparent failure of the Word of God to function as it is written in many people's lives. Is God the one who is to blame?

As we look at what we learned in the last chapter, and as we discuss this topic in this chapter, you will find the answer to be a resounding no. If no, then what is the problem? This is a major issue. For the majority of people that do not have even the most basic foundational understanding that God is always good, when asked if God is to blame for a tragedy, they assume He is. Again, because they know He has the power to stop bad things from happening, and apparently, He did not, they think He must have allowed it. But if you had the understanding that God is good and cannot lie, you would know the problem must lie elsewhere, and you would begin a quest to find the answer.

The disciples demonstrated this mind-set when they could not cast the demon out of the demon-possessed boy. Instead of asking, "Why did God choose to leave that demon there?" they asked Jesus, "Why couldn't we cast it out?"

This should be our immediate question when circumstances seem to contradict the Word of God. So again, it is vital that we must, first of all, know that God is good and, secondly, that He does not lie. This is also why I have spent so much time laying out what seems to me to be a no-brainer, but surprisingly, to most of the church world, is a mystery. Asking questions is how you must read the Bible if you want to learn how the Kingdom works.

THE KINGDOM OF GOD IS A KINGDOM AND OPERATES WITH LAWS AND PRINCIPLES THAT NEVER CHANGE.

Remember, those great Bible stories are there for a reason. Jesus is trying to show you something. So, let's move on to why someone did not receive what the Word of God said. Well, there could be many issues that are short-circuiting heaven's jurisdiction. Some issues are not immediately evident, and some are personal and hidden.

The Kingdom of God is a kingdom and operates with laws and principles that never change. Those principles, as I said, can be learned and used just as a farmer understands the laws of seedtime and harvest in the earth realm and uses those laws to prosper. Because the Kingdom operates by laws, which are given to every citizen to understand and use, anyone can learn them. Sometimes, knowing how these laws work can be life and death.

A Life and Death Decision

Mark and Hannah came to our church and desired to have a baby. Up until this time, Hannah was told by doctors that due to various issues in her body, it would be almost impossible for her to get pregnant or to carry a baby. But while hearing of the goodness of God and learning Kingdom law at Faith Life Church, she found out she was pregnant. She was thrilled beyond words. But before long, she began to have severe pain in her abdomen. A couple of times, it was so severe that she passed out.

After one of these episodes, she wanted to have things checked out and went to her doctor's office. Her doctor was not in, but the doctor on call wanted to do an ultrasound to see what was going on. What the doctor saw was a big blood clot, and he told her that she had miscarried, there was no heartbeat. The doctor offered to have her come in the following day to have her dead baby removed from her womb, but Hannah refused. Instead, her husband, Mark, encouraged Hannah with the Word of God and God's promises and encouraged her not to cast aside her confidence concerning the baby. That weekend, she received prayer at church and was convinced that she would have a healthy baby in spite of what the doctor had told her.

That Monday, she went in to see her personal doctor, as her doctor was not in the day she had stopped by the office. Her doctor suggested that she have another ultrasound. Hannah said the doctor had a shocked look on her face as she stared at the ultrasound screen and immediately looked at the scans that were done a few days earlier. Then she said the following words to Hannah: "I have been doing this for 30 years, and I have never seen this happen before. I can see the big blood clot on last week's scans and the absence of a heartbeat. As I look at you today, the entire blood clot is gone, and there is a perfect baby, alive, with a perfect heartbeat." A few months later, Hannah gave birth to a healthy baby girl, who she named Evelyn. Curious one day as to the meaning of the name Evelyn, she looked it up and was surprised that the name actually means life!

This amazing story was obviously the work of God, but as a spiritual scientist, you should be thinking of a few questions like these right now. Why did it happen? Is Hannah one of God's favorites? Did God just randomly choose to heal her baby? These are questions that must be answered. Again, to the average Christian, a miracle has taken place. But I encourage people to rethink the word miracle as it implies something out of the ordinary. In the Kingdom, this was simply a function of Kingdom law.

If I dropped a rock and it fell to the ground, you would think I was nuts if I yelled out, "Wow, did you see that? The rock just fell to the ground; that's a miracle!" You would disagree that it was a miracle because you know the action was simply the function of the law of gravity, and it works the same way every time for anyone. The rock will always fall to the ground. So as a spiritual scientist, you must look for clues as to what happened, spiritual clues that will reveal the law or laws of the Kingdom that were present in the story.

A Key Revealed

Let's move on to another story where we can learn more about the

Kingdom's function in regard to these questions. One of the greatest stories in the Bible that will help us find some answers is found in Luke chapter eight.

> *As Jesus was on his way, the crowds almost crushed him. And a woman was there who had been subject to bleeding for twelve years but no one could heal her. She came up behind him and touched the edge of his cloak, and immediately her bleeding stopped.*
>
> *"Who touched me?" Jesus asked.*
>
> *When they all denied it, Peter said, "Master, the people are crowding and pressing against you."*
>
> *But Jesus said, "Someone touched me; I know that power has gone out from me."*
>
> *Then the woman, seeing that she could not go unnoticed, came trembling and fell at his feet. In the presence of all the people, she told why she had touched him and how she had been instantly healed. Then he said to her, "Daughter, your faith has healed you. Go in peace."*
>
> —Luke 8:42-48

In this story, we find a woman who was very sick for many years and could not get well. Coming up behind Jesus, she touched His cloak and was immediately healed. Now, there are some very profound clues of the Kingdom's operation in this story that we can learn from and that will bring to light some of the answers we are looking for.

First of all, the crowd that was surrounding Jesus was all touching Him. As the story says, He was almost being crushed by the crowd that pressed against Him. When Jesus asked, "Who touched me?" Peter was amazed at the question because, again, everyone was touching Him. But Jesus said this particular person had touched Him in a different way as He had felt the power of the Holy Spirit flow out of Him.

After reading this story, all kinds of bells and whistles should be going off in your spirit urging you to stop and consider what had just happened. Your mind should have immediately launched into investigative mode with a myriad of questions. As spiritual scientists, we need to know why this woman was healed and no one else was. I can assume that there were many others there who were physically touching Him that were also sick yet not being healed. So we need to ask, "Why did the anointing flow only to this woman and not to everyone else who touched Him at that moment?"

The traditional religious answer is that she was healed because Jesus healed her. But did He? Was Jesus intentionally ministering to her when she was healed? Did He lay His hands on her? Did He command the sickness to leave her body? The answer is no. In fact, Jesus did not even know she was there. He had to ask who had touched Him. So did Jesus actually choose to heal her at that moment? Again, He did not even know she was there. So, how was she healed? Why was she healed?

As spiritual scientists, we can rule out the thought that she was one of God's special kids or that she had a special connection to Jesus, because Acts 10:34 (KJV) says that God is no respecter of persons. We can also assume that since Jesus did not even know she was there, He had no part in her decision to be healed that day. We do agree that He was the reservoir of the anointing, but He was not part of the decision she made to be healed at that moment.

Jesus tells us exactly how she tapped into the Kingdom's authority and power. He said, "Daughter, your faith has healed you. Go in peace." This sentence tells us everything we need to know and answers our question as to why and how she received that day. As spiritual scientists, let's begin to take a closer look at this story and see if we can pick up any clues as to why she received.

First of all, Jesus calls her daughter, meaning she was part of the nation of Israel, a descendant of Abraham. As a child of Abraham, she possessed the blessing given to Abraham and the benefits of the covenant that God made with Abraham.

> He said, "If you listen carefully to the Lord your God and do what is right in his eyes, if you pay attention to his commands and keep all his decrees, I will not bring on you any of the diseases I brought on the Egyptians, for I am the Lord, who heals you."
> —Exodus 15:26

So when Jesus called her daughter, that meant she had a legal right to all that was included in Abraham's covenant that he made with God. However, this fact alone cannot be the only reason she received as everyone there that day that was pressing against Jesus had that same legality. There had to be something else that had caused the power of the Kingdom of God to flow. Jesus then tells us one more reason she received. In fact, Jesus said this was the exact reason she personally received. He said her faith had healed her.

So, now we know the reasons she was able to receive. It was legally her right to receive since she was a daughter of Abraham, and secondly, her faith was the switch that allowed that power to flow personally into her body at that exact moment. The fact that she was a daughter can be compared to the power company having the power on and the wires coming into your home. The power is available, but that does not mean your lights will be on. You must also flip the switch to on before the lights will come on.

So as a legal descendent of Abraham, this woman had a legal right to be healed. However, because she had jurisdiction on the earth and over her own life, she had to personally turn on the switch to release that power. But where is the switch? How do we turn it on? To find out, we need to define our terms.

What Is Faith?

Faith is a term that Christians throw around loosely. And I am convinced that many, if not the majority, do not know what faith actually is, why it is needed, how to know if they are in faith, and how to obtain faith. If faith is the switch that allowed the anointing to flow to and heal this woman, then we need to take

FAITH IS A TERM THAT CHRISTIANS THROW AROUND LOOSELY.

a very close look at faith! We find our definition of faith in Romans 4:18–21.

> *Against all hope, Abraham in hope believed and so became the father of many nations, just as it had been said to him, "So shall your offspring be." Without weakening in his faith, he faced the fact that his body was as good as dead—since he was about a hundred years old—and that Sarah's womb was also dead. Yet he did not waver through unbelief regarding the promise of God, but was strengthened in his faith and gave glory to God, being*

fully persuaded that God had power to do what he had promised.

—Romans 4:18-21

Let's understand the setting of this story. Abraham and Sarah could not have children. I do not mean they were having trouble conceiving a child and should have kept trying. I mean they were almost 100 years old, and it was over. Their bodies could not have children; it was impossible! Yet God promised Abraham a child even though in the natural, it was utterly impossible. The Bible says that Abraham was fully persuaded that God had the power to do what He said in spite of the natural facts that stated a different story.

Here then is our definition of faith: "being fully persuaded that God had the power to do what he had promised." I state it this way: "**your heart being in agreement with heaven**." That's not just agreeing mentally with what God says but being fully persuaded.

Our definition of what faith is:

Let me say it one more time to be sure we have this. Faith is being fully persuaded of what God says! It is our hearts and minds being in agreement with heaven, fully persuaded.

Why Is Faith Needed?

Why can't God heal everyone in the hospital when He wants to? Why can't He stop wars? Why can't He send angels to preach the Gospel to us? I am sure you have heard all of these questions before. The answer is that He can't. It is not that God does not have the power to do so, but He does not have the jurisdiction to do so. To understand what I am saying, we need to look at Hebrews 2:6-8.

But there is a place where someone has testified:
> *"What is mankind that you are mindful of them, a son of man that you care for him? You made them a little lower than the angels; you crowned them with glory and honor and put everything under their feet."*

In putting everything under them, God left nothing that is not subject to them. Yet at present we do not see everything subject to them.

—Hebrews 2:6-8

God gave man complete legal jurisdiction over the entire earth realm when he was placed here. There was nothing that was not under his jurisdiction. He ruled over this realm with absolute jurisdiction and authority. His ability to rule with authority was backed up by the government which had set him here. In essence, he ruled with the delegated authority of the Kingdom of God. He wore the crown of that government, which represented the glory of God, the anointing, and the position of honor or authority that he bore.

Now, of course, he did not really wear a real, metal crown, but yet he did have a crown in the sense of what a crown speaks of. To get a good picture of what this looks like, think of a natural king. Although he is a natural man and bears no real power in his natural being, he wears a crown, which signifies he stands in representation of not only himself but of an entire kingdom and government. His words carry authority only because they are backed up by all the power and natural resources of the government and the kingdom he represents.

If you think of a sheriff directing traffic, he will stop a massive tractor-trailer truck with a statement, "Stop in the name of the law."

Yes, the truck is much bigger than the man—and the man, in himself, is no match for the truck—but the truck stops, not because of the man but because of the badge that the man wears, which represents a government. In this case, the government is much bigger than the man who wears the badge. For the truck driver, there is no fear of the man, but there is a fear of the government which the man represents, causing the truck driver to stop.

The same is true here. Adam ruled over everything that was created in the earth realm. God's power and dominion, represented by the crown of glory and honor, gave man the assurance that his words ruled on behalf of the Kingdom of God.

It is very important to note that when Adam lost his ability to rule over the earth by committing treason against God's government, he lost his crown, his position of authority in the Kingdom of God, but he did not lose his legal claim on the earth realm itself. Man was still legally in charge of the earth. God had given it to him to rule over. If we go back to our text in Hebrews, we can see this.

> *But there is a place where someone has testified:*
>> *"What is mankind that you are mindful of them, a son of man that you care for him? You made them a little lower than the angels; you crowned them with glory and honor and put everything under their feet."*
>
> *In putting everything under them, God left nothing that is not subject to them. Yet at present we do not see everything subject to them.*
>
> *—Hebrews 2:6-8*

Even though this text is speaking of the time when Adam and

Eve were created, the text says, "God left nothing that is not subject to them."

> The highest heavens belong to the Lord, but the earth he has **given to mankind**.
>
> —Psalm 115:16

Man Kicked God Out

Even though man has the legal jurisdiction over the earth, he has lost his authority to rule spiritually. Essentially, Adam kicked God out of the affairs of men back in the Garden; and at the Fall, the earth realm became tainted and changed. Death entered the earth realm, and Satan now had a legal claim of influence in the affairs of men. But even though all this happened, it is imperative that you understand that man is still the legal occupant of the earth.

THIS IS WHY GOD HAS TO USE SPIRIT-FILLED PEOPLE TO BRING ABOUT HIS WILL IN THE LIVES OF MEN.

Even in his fallen state, he is still in charge. Yes, he no longer has his crown of God's government to back him up. He has no authority to rule with God's power and glory, and he has lost his position of honor. But he is still the only living being that has a legal right to rule over the earth realm.

This is why God has to use Spirit-filled people to bring about His will in the lives of men. In the same way, Satan uses demon inspired people to affect the earth realm toward his plan for man. This principle of man's jurisdiction over the earth is vital to your understanding of Kingdom law and, especially, why faith is required for God to gain legal jurisdiction in a situation.

You may say, "But I thought God owned the earth and the fullness there of?" True, He does. I hope this example will help you understand what I am saying. If I lease a home that I own to you, although I legally own the home, I legally give up the right to drop by anytime I want to. There is a clause in most leases that specifies when landlords may legally enter rented premises—for example, to deal with an emergency or make repairs—and the amount of notice required. If I try to enter the home outside of this agreement, it would be considered breaking and entering, even if I own the property. If I violate the law as specified in the lease, I could then legally be forced to vacate the premises even though I own the home.

This illustrates why Satan had to go through Adam to gain access to the earth realm. Only Adam had the key! Satan had to go through the door and had to have been given the key from the one who legally possessed it or he would legally have been forced out.

In this same way, once Adam kicked God's government out of the earth realm, God had to find a way to legally bring His government back into the earth realm. Again, he had to go through man. In this case, it was a man named Abram who opened the door.

> *The Lord had said to Abram, "Go from your country, your people and your father's household to the land I will show you. I will make you into a great nation, and I will bless you; I will make your name great, and you will be a blessing. I will bless those who bless you, and whoever curses you I will curse; and <u>all peoples on earth will be blessed through you</u>."*
>
> —Genesis 12:1-3

Abraham is called the father of our faith because he is the man that opened the door of the earth realm to God whereby all nations on the earth would be blessed. Of course, this is speaking of Jesus Christ and God's rescue plan for mankind. Abraham's faith opened a legal doorway which God permanently locked open by making a legal agreement between Abraham and Himself. This agreement was also binding to Abraham's seed, and this is what was meant in Genesis 12 when the Bible says, "all peoples on earth will be blessed through you." "Blessed through you" is referring to Jesus coming through the lineage of Abraham and restoring what Adam lost.

So let me paraphrase what I am saying. A man or woman who has legal jurisdiction in the earth realm must stand in agreement with heaven for heaven to have legal access into the earth realm. This agreement with heaven is called faith. This is the same principle whereby Satan gained legal access into the earth realm through a man who held the key, Adam.

> *The devil led him [jesus] up to a high place and showed him in an instant all the kingdoms of the world. And he said to him, "I will give you all their authority and splendor; it has been given to me, and I can give it to anyone I want to. If you worship me, it will all be yours."*
>
> —Luke 4:5-7

You can see in this verse that Satan claims that the authority and splendor (wealth) of the kingdoms of men have been given to him. He claims absolute authority over the earth as it pertains to mankind. So who gave him this authority? The one who had it, which was Adam! Thus God cannot just burst into the affairs of men without a legal entrance, or it would be illegal. Satan would claim foul play. No, God has to go through the same door that Satan did, through a man or woman on the earth.

Jesus Couldn't Heal Them—A Powerful Lesson Uncovered

> *Jesus said to them, "A prophet is not without honor except in his own town, among his relatives and in his own home."* **<u>He could not do any miracles there</u>**, *except lay his hands on a few sick people and heal them. He was amazed at their lack of faith.*
> —Mark 6:4-6

If I asked people on the street if Jesus could do anything, they would probably say He could. If I then asked if there was anyplace in the Bible where Jesus tried but could not do miracles, what would they say? I assure you they would tell me that there was no such place in the Bible. But yet, you just read one. Jesus could not heal them. As a spiritual scientist, I want to know why. The answer is simply that He couldn't, and now you know why. It was because they had no faith, which means there was no agreement with heaven, and thus heaven had no legal jurisdiction in that situation. Make sure you have a clear understanding of what we have discovered.

Heaven has no jurisdiction on the earth unless a man or woman's heart is fully persuaded of what heaven says, which is called FAITH.

If we go back to the questions I asked in the first part of this chapter about unanswered prayer, we can get our answers now. Remember, I mentioned a possible situation where millions of people could be praying for someone and they would still die. Why? The primary reason is, again, no faith. Most people are mistaking a lot of noise for faith.

And when you pray, do not keep on babbling like pagans, for they think they will be heard because of their many words. Do not be like them, for your Father knows what you need before you ask him.

—Matthew 6:7–8

A lot of people believe that the more people that are praying, the greater the chance of God hearing and being moved to help. I hope we have covered enough by now that you know this is completely false. And when we say there was no faith, primarily, we are talking about the one who needs to receive from God having faith.

In our story in Mark chapter 6, you would have to agree that Jesus had plenty of faith, yet He could not heal them. So if you and I were talking about the sick friend with millions praying, I would ask you, "What is the sick man saying?" You see, no amount of people have spiritual authority over another person. We could have 20 billion people praying for someone, but if that person is not in faith and is saying they are going to die, they will die.

Again, let's consider our example we just looked at in Mark 6. We know that Jesus had faith to heal, but He could not do anything for the people without their faith being engaged.

I have had numerous people come to me stating that their grandmother or their grandfather or a relative is sick and say that they have been praying for them, but yet nothing is happening. I always ask, "What is the grandmother saying? What is the grandfather saying? Is there faith there?" You see, you do not have spiritual authority over another person. You can minister to them, but they have to be engaged in that. So what I tell people they must do if they want to see effective ministry is to first change the picture. I am talking about the picture the sick person sees about their own situation. Do not give them a lot of religious quotes; give them a picture. Let me show you what I am talking about.

> *John's disciples told him about all these things. Calling two of them, he sent them to the Lord to ask, "Are you the one who is to come, or should we expect someone else?"*
>
> *When the men came to Jesus, they said, "John the Baptist sent us to you to ask, 'Are you the one who is to come, or should we expect someone else?'"*
>
> *At that very time Jesus cured many who had diseases, sicknesses and evil spirits, and gave sight to many who were blind. So he replied to the messengers, "Go back and report to John what you have seen and heard: The blind receive sight, the lame walk, those who have leprosy are cleansed, the deaf hear, the dead are raised, and the good news is proclaimed to the poor."*
>
> —Luke 7:18-22

Notice Jesus did not refer to a Scripture. He could have said, "You go back and tell John this Scripture or that Scripture." But no, He told them about all the good things that were happening by the Kingdom of God. You would do the same. Tell your friend who is sick a story of how Jesus healed someone else. If possible, tell them a story about someone that was healed from

"CONSEQUENTLY, FAITH COMES FROM HEARING THE MESSAGE, AND THE MESSAGE IS HEARD THROUGH THE WORD ABOUT CHRIST."

—ROMANS 10:17

the exact same disease that is afflicting their body. This picture will inspire them and bring hope. Hope always carries a picture with it, and this is the picture you want your friend to see, that there is healing for that disease.

Once your friend sees that it is possible to be healed, they will then ask you how that is possible. This is the moment you have been waiting for. Instead of preaching at them, they are now open to receiving instruction regarding the Word of God and the principles of the Kingdom. First, you will want to bring them into the Kingdom if they are not born again; and secondly, you will need to spend some time with them explaining the Scriptures regarding healing. If possible, leave them some material to reinforce what you have told them.

We now know what faith is (agreement with heaven) and why faith is legally required, but we still need to know how to get faith and how to know if we are in faith.

How Do We Get in Faith?

Consequently, faith comes from hearing the message, and the message is heard through the word about Christ.
—Romans 10:17

How does faith come by hearing the Word of God? What is the process? Is just hearing the Word all it takes for faith to be developed in the human spirit? To understand how faith comes and what Romans 10:17 is talking about, we can look to Mark chapter 4. I always say if you throw your Bible up in the air, it should land open to Mark chapter 4; it is that important! Jesus said in Mark 4:13 that if you did not understand what He was teaching in that chapter, you would not be able to understand any other parable in the Bible. I would say that is pretty important!

Why is this chapter so important? Because it tells us how heaven interfaces with the earth realm, how it gains jurisdiction, and where that takes place. Nothing is more important to your life than knowing what this whole chapter is talking about.

In this chapter, Jesus tells us three parables regarding how faith is produced in the human spirit, which is, as you know now, a requirement for heaven to legally invade Earth. The three stories in this chapter are the parable of the sower, the parable of the man scattering seed, and the story of the mustard seed. Let's start by looking at the second story Jesus tells in Mark chapter 4, the story of the man scattering seed.

> He also said, "This is what the kingdom of God is like. A man scatters seed on the ground. Night and day, whether he sleeps or gets up, the seed sprouts and grows, though he does not know how. All by itself the soil produces grain—first the stalk, then the head, then the full kernel in the head. As soon as the grain is ripe, he puts the sickle to it, because the harvest has come."
>
> —Mark 4:26–29

The first thing we need to do is to define our terms. What is the seed Jesus is talking about and what is the ground? Jesus actually defines those two terms in the preceding parable of the sower in the same chapter. The seed is the Word of God, and the ground is the heart of man or the spirit of man.

So in this parable, Jesus says a man scatters the Word of God into his heart. Then all by itself, the soil, or the heart of man, starts to produce faith, or agreement, with heaven. Now, this is the natural process and function of your human spirit. It is going to incubate what you put in there. Before I go forward, it is critical that you remember what our definition of faith is: the heart of a man or a woman firmly persuaded of what heaven says. Now, the tricky thing to remember here is agreement with heaven is not the same thing as mentally agreeing with the Word of God. The Bible says that Abraham was fully persuaded.

Fully Persuaded

To help you get a clear picture of what fully persuaded looks and feels like, let's say I told you to jump from the top of the Empire State building in New York City. To convince you to try it, I told you that if you flapped your arms hard enough, you could fly safely down to Earth. You would laugh in my face because you KNEW what would happen to you. You were fully persuaded of the result. That is what fully persuaded feels like. You know you are persuaded; there is no other possibility. You would die if you jumped.

So let's take another situation and see how you do with it. Let's assume that you have a very visible, large lump on your body, and the doctor says you have about one month to live: you have cancer. In fact, the doctor says that your form of cancer is so rare that there is no one that has actually lived that has been diagnosed with it. Now, let's assume you know what 1 Peter 2:24 says.

> *He himself bore our sins in his body on the cross, so that we might die to sins and live for righteousness; by his wounds you have been healed.*
>
> —1 Peter 2:24

The Scripture tells us the answer, but you and I have a serious problem. We grew up in the kingdom of darkness, and perversion and death were all around us. We have grown up in the kingdom of fear, being fully persuaded of what fear says. So in the above illustration, we have been trained that cancer can kill. We have evidence in every media broadcast that this is true. So how are we going to change our agreement; how can we become fully persuaded of what God says? Well, in reality, we can't by ourselves. But the Word of God is alive and full of power, and by planting it in your spirit, all by itself, your spirit and the Word begin to produce agreement with what heaven says.

Agreement with Heaven

He also said, "This is what the kingdom of God is like. A man scatters seed on the ground. Night and day, whether he sleeps or gets up, the seed sprouts and grows, though he does not know how. All by itself the soil produces grain—first the stalk, then the head, then the full kernel in the head. As soon as the grain is ripe, he puts the sickle to it, because the harvest has come."

—Mark 4:26-29

All by itself, the soil (your heart) produces agreement. Notice you cannot pray for faith; it is a function of your heart and the Word. As we look at this text, we can see that the agreement of our heart with heaven is a process; it does not happen instantly.

This illustration tells us that at first when our heart receives the Word, faith starts to grow, just like a blade or sprout of a newly planted seed grows. It then goes on and continues to grow as a stalk, and then it forms the head. The head is where the seed or fruit is beginning to form. At this phase of the plant's life, you still have nothing to eat. The plant has not produced its mature, ripe fruit yet, but it is growing.

So it is with the Word of God. There is no visible change yet in the natural realm when faith is growing. There is not agreement yet, but be assured the plant is growing, faith is being produced, and agreement is happening. Jesus goes on to explain that when the seed in the head is fully mature or ripe, the harvest has come, agreement is there, and now faith is there.

So here is the understanding. When you plant a seed in the ground, through the process of germination, the plant starts to grow, but there is no fruit yet. The plant continues growing as long as it stays in the right environment; and as it matures, it shoots out its fruit. Let's say you are growing corn. The corn plant shoots out a corn ear, but at first, it is just a small ear of corn with no ripe corn that you could eat. But after a season, the corn on the ear becomes mature and ripe. Now catch this point! At the moment the kernel of corn on the ear matches the kernel of corn that was sown into the ground, there is agreement.

When the seed that is in the head of the plant matures, it will look exactly—EXACTLY—like the seed that was sown.

Plant a corn plant, and the mature seed in the ear will match the seed that you planted. They are the same. They look the same and taste the same; you cannot tell them apart.

So let me paraphrase what Jesus is saying. When we hear the Word of God (Romans 10:17), we are actually scattering God's Word into our spirit men, our hearts. If we keep that Word in our hearts, it will grow and mature; and when it is mature, our hearts will be fully persuaded of what heaven said. Heaven and earth match, and heaven has now gained legal jurisdiction in the earth realm through the person that is fully persuaded. Our thoughts and belief exactly match what heaven says with full confidence. This is not a mental thing. This has now become what we actually believe just as sure as we believe a rock will fall if dropped. Heaven sows the Word into the earth realm where it will bring about agreement and God's will. If heaven says you are healed, then when that Word matures in your heart, all you will see is what heaven says. No more fear. When you close your eyes, you will see yourself healed! This is why Hebrews 11:1 (KJV) says:

> Now faith is the substance of things hoped for, the <u>evidence of things not seen</u>.

You may not see it yet in the natural, but you have seen it in your spirit, and it is just as real as if you were holding it in your hand. That agreement is called faith, and that faith will bring that picture to pass here in the earth realm, in your life!

Flipping the Switch

But hold on; this is not where Mark chapter four stops. After it teaches us how our hearts come into agreement with heaven and faith is there, it gives us instruction on how to harvest that fruit.

> As soon as the grain is ripe, **he puts the sickle to it**, because the harvest has come.
>
> —Mark 4:29

Notice that even though the heart is in agreement with heaven and there is faith, nothing happens yet. Why? As we have been saying all along, you have the legal jurisdiction here in the earth realm. Do you remember our discussion on Luke 8 regarding the woman with the issue of blood? Remember Jesus said, "Daughter, your faith has healed you"? I told you then that daughter inferred a legal standing before heaven, that because she was a daughter of Abraham, she had legal rights.

I compared it to having the wires from the power plant connected to your house. The power is there and available, but you still have to personally turn on the lights. This is the same. Once faith is established, the power is available, but nothing happens yet because you have to turn the switch on. You have to release the power of the Kingdom of God here in the earth realm because only you, a man or woman on the earth, can legally do it. This principle is exactly how you were saved, as mentioned in Romans 10:10.

YOU HAVE TO RELEASE THE POWER OF THE KINGDOM OF GOD HERE IN THE EARTH REALM BECAUSE ONLY YOU, A MAN OR WOMAN ON THE EARTH, CAN LEGALLY DO IT.

> *For it is with your heart that you believe and are justified, and it is with your mouth that you profess your faith and are saved.*
> —Romans 10:10

With the heart man believes the Word and is justified. Justify is a legal term meaning the administration of law. So when a man or woman's heart is in agreement with heaven, when they believe what heaven says, they are justified before heaven and Earth. It is now legal for heaven to flow into their lives and through their lives and to impact the earth on behalf of the Kingdom of God. But strangely, even though it is now legal and they are in faith, still nothing happens. "But, Gary, I thought you said if I was in faith, it gave heaven legal jurisdiction here." Correct, but someone has to release heaven's authority here once faith exists. Let's look at our Scripture one more time.

> *For it is with your heart that you believe and are justified,* ***and it is with your mouth that you profess your faith and are saved***.
>
> —Romans 10:10

Once you are in faith, or justified, it is now legal for heaven to invade Earth, but notice that it then says that it is with your mouth that you confess and are saved. Do you see the two parts? Heaven's part is bringing the Word into your heart where it incubates agreement here in the earth realm. Then once agreement or faith is there, you must act on that agreement and release the authority of heaven into your situation to actually receive what heaven says. In our Scripture in Mark 4:29, it says when the harvest is come, the man (on the earth) puts the sickle in. He is the one that has to act on the Word of God once faith is there and actually receive that harvest.

Receiving in God's Kingdom

Let me go back and talk about the sickle here in Mark four for a moment. I believe that most of the church world has not been taught how to use the sickle, meaning they have not been taught how to harvest what they need. I did not know this either until the Lord began teaching me how the Kingdom operated. Here's the story of how my first revelation of this vital process in the Kingdom happened.

I was invited to speak at a church in Atlanta. It was a Wednesday night service; and the church was not that big, but that was fine with me. I just loved teaching people about the Kingdom. As I arrived at the church, I found it strange that the doors were locked and no one was there. It was ten minutes before service was to begin. I heard a really loud truck behind me, and as I looked over, I saw an old pickup truck pulling in behind the alley of the church. I thought nothing of it; after all, I was in downtown Atlanta.

As I waited, a man came walking from behind the building and introduced himself as the pastor. He said he was sorry for being late, but his old truck would not start. He told me he had to start it by rolling it down a hill as the clutch was out. He went on to say that sometimes it would not start at all, and he would be forced to walk the five miles to church. I will have to admit that I was a little surprised by this conversation.

He went on to explain that this church really was primarily an outreach ministry and that he fed thousands of people every month, usually totaling over 10,000 meals a month, from that one location. As the pastor was speaking, I was getting upset. Here is a man of God who is feeding 10,000 people a month, and he does not even have a decent car? I could take care of that. I had a fairly young car with 20,000 miles on it at home that I would give him. I told him of my plan and that I would send one of my staff down to Atlanta with the car. He, of course, was thrilled.

I spent that night teaching him and his small church about the

Kingdom of God and how it functioned in relation to money. I knew it was vital that they begin to demonstrate what the Kingdom looked like to those who so desperately needed it.

When I went home, I arranged for the car to be driven to Atlanta. When my staff member came to pick up the car, I knew that I was making a spiritual transaction in heaven. I knew that as I released that car into the Kingdom of God, I could believe God for a vehicle that I would have need of as well. I am not a car person, meaning I am not really into cars. Some people are, but I am not. So I laid my hand on that car as my staff member came to pick it up, and I basically said, "Father, I release this car into this assignment in Atlanta. As I release it, I sow it as a seed and believe that I receive a _____." I could not think of a car that I wanted. So I said, "I will get back to you on that!"

Well, over the next couple of months, I really did not think much about a car, but one morning, I asked Drenda what kind of car she would like to have. After she thought for a bit, she said that a convertible would be nice. Well, I asked her what kind of convertible did she want, and neither of us could think of any models that were out there. Since I was buying the car for Drenda, I wanted to be sure that she got the car she liked. I told her to check online or look around and let me know if she found a convertible she would like. We did not tell anyone about our desire for a new car, but meanwhile, we kept our eyes open as we drove around, looking for a car that might catch our attention.

One day, we were pulling in to a local restaurant for lunch, and suddenly, Drenda yelled out, "There it is!" "There what is?" I asked. "The car I like." She was pointing across the parking lot, so I drove around the lot and pulled in behind a BMW 6 Series Ci convertible, a beautiful car for sure. And might I add an expensive car as well. I complimented her on her taste and told her that it was a beautiful car.

Now, you need to know that Drenda and I do not go out and pay big bucks for cars. As I said, I have never really been a car guy. Being in finance, I also knew how fast they depreciate and that it was always best to buy a car that was one to two years old. So that was my plan; I would look for a great used one.

Well, a week later, a guy from the church calls me and says these words, "I found Drenda's car!" I was puzzled as we had not told anyone about the BMW we saw that day at lunch. So I asked him what kind of car it was, and he said it was a BMW 6 Series Ci convertible. He said as he was driving around, he saw it, and the Lord told him it was Drenda's car. "Okay, now you have my attention," I told him. The car was one year old and in mint condition. I ended up paying cash for it, and Drenda got her car.

Wow, how did that happen?

Let's compare the story to what we learned about being in faith and putting the sickle in. When I gave my car away, I was in faith. But when Drenda said out loud, "That's it!" she was putting the sickle in, then a few days later, the car showed up. Although I heard her say out loud, "That's it!" I never tied her declaration to Mark chapter four and the sickle. But this next story made it crystal clear.

The Power of Your Words

As I said, I own 60 acres with about 10 acres of it being marsh. I love to hunt in the fall, and even though I had hunted ducks back in high school, I really had not done any duck hunting here in Ohio. But that year, the marsh was full of water, and big flocks of ducks just kept flying into it. Hundreds a day would come in to roost at night. So I grabbed my shotgun one night and went out and had a great time shooting a few ducks for dinner.

That fall, both my boys and I enjoyed some good duck hunting. One thing I noticed, however, was that a lot of the time, the ducks were at my maximum shotgun range. When hunting ducks, you are only legally allowed to use steel shot as opposed to the traditional lead shot. Lead shot is heavier and retains its energy much farther out than steel shot, thus the problem with shooting long-range while duck hunting.

But during that fall as I was talking to a few fellow duck hunters, they told me about these new guns that were designed just for duck hunting. They were able to shoot heavier shot loads and were camouflage as well. I was very interested in possibly buying one, but it was December, duck season was closing, and I did not think much more about it.

In early January, I happened to stop by Cabela's (our local sporting goods store) for something, and I remembered those duck guns. I wanted to see one. So I walked past the gun counter on the way out, and I saw a complete section of new guns dedicated to water fowl hunting. I remember, without thinking about it, pointing my finger at the one I thought looked the best and saying out loud. "Lord, I will have that one." I had not thought about it as I said it; it just came out of my mouth. The duck season did not open again until fall, so I was not planning on buying the gun until the season got a little closer.

Two weeks later, I was invited to speak at a business conference. As I finished, the CEO came out to thank me and said they had bought a gift for me. And amazingly, he brought out the exact gun, the exact model, I had pointed at two weeks earlier in Cabela's. I was, of course, totally surprised by such a generous gift, but I knew this was not a coincidence. I remembered then what I had said while at the Cabela's store and realized what I had done. I had put the sickle in!

> He also said, "This is what the kingdom of God is like. A man scatters seed on the ground. Night and day, whether he sleeps or gets up, the seed sprouts and grows, though he does not know how. All by itself the soil produces grain—first the stalk, then the head, then the full kernel in the head. As soon as the grain is ripe, <u>he puts the sickle to it, because the harvest has come.</u>"
>
> —Mark 4:26-29

Putting the sickle in illustrates the same principle regarding faith that we discussed earlier in Romans 10:10.

> For it is with your heart that you believe and are justified, and it is with your mouth that you profess your faith and are saved.
>
> —Romans 10:10

With my heart I believed, and it was with my mouth that I had released the Kingdom in the earth realm. I had given over 30 guns away, but this was the first time that I actually remember saying out loud, "I will take that one." But as I thought about it for a minute, there was only one other time I had done the same thing—but at that time, I had no clue how the Kingdom operated.

When Drenda and I moved back to Ohio, we came from Oklahoma where deer hunting was done with a rifle. But in Ohio, rifles were not legal; only shotguns using slugs were allowed. All I had at the time was that 20-gauge double barrel with which I managed to harvest two deer the first year we moved. But I really wanted a good shotgun that was designed specifically to hunt deer with. I remembered that after that first deer season in Ohio, I had commented to Drenda that I really wanted a Remington model 11-87 12-gauge with a black synthetic stock for deer hunting. Christmas was a few weeks later, and I was surprised when my dad gave me that exact shotgun for Christmas. I had not even mentioned to him my need for a shotgun. I remember thinking, "Boy, that was weird." I had put the sickle in without knowing it.

CHAPTER 4
DON'T YOU REMEMBER?

In the early days when I was first learning how the Kingdom worked, I was shocked at the things I saw. It was mainly because I had never been taught any of the things I was seeing. But as I said in the first part of the book, God seemed to use my deer hunting for many of the lessons He was teaching me. I am basically a fairly simple person, and I guess that was a great way to catch my attention. After I learned how to sow for my deer and began harvesting them—usually within about 40 minutes after going out, God began to fine-tune my lessons as greater insights into the Kingdom's function.

I was in Tulsa, Oklahoma, when God showed me how to hunt by faith for that six-point buck. And as I told you, we moved back to Ohio the following year. Ohio had a large deer herd and allowed you to take two deer of which only one could be a buck. So when I came to Ohio, I started sowing for two deer, one buck and one doe each year. And like clockwork, that is what I got.

But one year, I noticed something that puzzled me. I thought, "No, this could not be happening." As I finished up that deer season, I noticed that the deer came in the order that I had written them down on my check when I sowed my seed. For instance, if I wrote "for a buck and a doe," the buck came first and the doe second. As I reflected on the past few seasons in Ohio, I thought this was happening every year. I was not sure as I had never paid much attention to it, but for some reason, I wondered if this was true.

So the next year, I knew I had to find out. I agree it was a crazy thought, but I thought it seemed to be working this way, and I would never know unless I did a few experiments. So I reversed the order when I sowed my seed that year. This time, I put the doe first on the list. Until then I always wrote the buck first when sowing my seed. Sure enough, that was exactly the order they came in. So the next year, I did it again, and they came in the order that I wrote them down. I had never even thought something like this could be happening. I mean, was the Kingdom that specific?

To find out if this was actually happening or just a coincidence, I decided to find out for sure and to run an experiment that was a little more in-depth. That year, I sowed my seed for a seven-point buck. I knew that a normal, typical deer would have even points on each side, so I picked an odd number and an exact number. So that is what Drenda and I sowed for, as strange as this may sound. We prayed and released our seed for a seven-point buck.

How Specific Is Faith?

October finally came around, and bow season opened. Usually, I couldn't wait to get in the woods with my bow, but I noticed that I felt strange as the season opened. I had no desire to go out. The feeling was strong and, weirdly, I knew I just couldn't go out yet. At the time, I thought that this lack of desire to go hunting would lift as the season went on and the leaves began to fall. But nope, I just could not explain it; I had no desire to go out, none. I remember thinking, "Is this what happens when you get older, you just stop doing things?" I mean I could not explain this strange feeling I had. It was like I couldn't have cared less if I ever went deer hunting again. Well, now it was November, and I was getting a bit concerned. I had already missed the most beautiful time in the woods and the warmest, I might add. It was then the middle of November, and I still had absolutely no desire to go out deer hunting. I wondered if I would even go out at all; that is how it felt.

Drenda's parents had driven up from Alabama to stay with us for a couple of days. As we were sitting around talking in the living room, all of a sudden, I knew that I needed to be out in the woods the next day. It was like a switch had been turned on. I told all of them that I had to go out in the morning to get my buck. All of a sudden, I was excited and expectant as I got my gear ready for the next morning.

I knew that my seven-point buck was going to be there. And then I understood. The seven-point must not have been there in October, and he was not there the day before. That must have been the reason I felt so blah about deer hunting. I can imagine how hard it would have been waiting a month and a half if I was just looking out my window wishing I was out there every day for a month and a half. That would have been depressing. At this point, the whole thing was just a theory, but I was about to test it the next morning.

It was dark as I got up that morning, and I had prayed during the night as to which tree stand I should head to. I have several stands on my property, and as I prayed about it, I felt for certain I was to go to the marsh stand. We call it the marsh stand because it borders about ten acres of marsh on one side of the stand with brush on the other side of the stand. I knew that deer would sometimes make their way around the marsh by going along the edge. The stand had paid off in the past, and I fully expected to see my buck at the marsh stand that day.

As I made my way to the stand, I reviewed what God had shown me in the past regarding His Kingdom through deer hunting, and I felt He was teaching me more. I was excited to see the result of my experiment.

The morning light slowly came up, and the usual sounds and smells of a fall morning were a welcome change of pace for me. I really had missed it. It was almost an hour into the morning, and there was no sign of deer. Yet I knew from watching the deer pattern on my property that the deer came into this area later in the morning as it was a prime bedding area. Although I had been in the stand for about an hour, legal shooting light had only been available for about 40 minutes.

As I sat there, I heard a car door slam up at the house. Then I remembered that Drenda's parents were leaving that morning to drive back to Alabama, and I wanted to say good-bye to them. So, reluctantly, I got down out of my stand, thinking that I would just have to come out another day for my seven-point.

As I got to the house, everyone was up and ready for breakfast. I am always the breakfast cook in the family, cooking breakfast almost every day for Drenda and myself and whoever else is there. So I went to work cooking breakfast as Drenda's parents finished packing their car. Of course, they asked about my buck, and I had to tell them that I decided to abandon my plan so I could spend the morning with them. Yes, I was a little disappointed. I had anticipated that they would be leaving a bit later in the morning, leaving me time to bag my buck.

But as I was standing over the stove top stirring some scrambled eggs, I glanced out the kitchen window which faced our back woods and fields. I spotted a buck chasing a doe across the backside of the field, heading directly for the marsh area where my stand was. I just knew that had to be my buck. I suddenly yelled out loud for someone to take over cooking and said I just saw my buck, and I was going to go and get him. I knew I did not have much time.

I would have to run around the property from the opposite direction to avoid being spotted by the buck. I figured he might just be headed down the trail my stand was on. I ran as fast as I could around the field and got to the stand without seeing any deer, which was good. I knew then that I had beat them there if, in fact, they would choose to come down my trail. I quickly climbed up into the stand with my heart racing and with sweat pouring down my face.

Suddenly, just as I sat down, there they came. The doe came trotting by directly below my stand, and I readied myself as I knew the buck was not far behind. Sure enough, there he came. I had no time to verify if he was indeed a seven-point or not. I barely had time to get my bow up to take the shot. At the shot, I knew that I hit the buck but had hit just a bit low, which concerned me. The buck jumped into the weeds at the shot. I waited in the stand for about 20 minutes and finally made my way down the tree, eager to check the arrow for signs of a hit. Unfortunately, there was very little blood on the arrow and the ground.

I was a little upset with my shot, but I knew the buck would bed down in the weeds, and I did not want to push him out just yet. I have shot bucks before with very little blood and knew the best thing was to let them sit for a while. So I went back up to the house and finished breakfast, told everyone the story, and then told my boys how I needed them to help me walk the field to see if we could find the buck. My hope was that we would find the buck had been hit better than the arrow indicated and that it might have already died. But I knew there was always a chance that I had hit too low and the buck was just wounded.

After waiting a couple of hours, we went out, and the three of us spread out across the field. I had my bow cocked and ready if I needed it. Suddenly, on the far side of the field, Tim jumped the buck. It had not seen me and was running in my direction. As it ran, it suddenly saw Tom, and it came to a stop to get a bearing on which way to go.

The buck was about 65 to 70 yards away, too far for a good crossbow shot with the lower powered crossbows of that day, but I knew that was my only chance. I quickly raised the bow and aimed over the top of the deer and let the arrow go. In amazement, the arrow arched toward the buck and hit it squarely in the center of its neck. It bolted down the hill out of sight. I was stunned. Wow. We slowly moved in the direction the buck had run, and I saw it lying down about 100 yards ahead of us. It had its head up but had not seen us, so we backed up and decided to come back later.

YES, THE KINGDOM WAS THAT SPECIFIC! NO ONE EVER TOLD ME THAT THE KINGDOM WORKED LIKE THIS, THAT THE KINGDOM WAS THAT SPECIFIC, AND THAT WE ACTUALLY HAD THAT KIND OF AUTHORITY.

Well, later was really much later as I had a full day ahead of me at church and was not able to get back home until after dark. Tim and I grabbed a flashlight and went back to where we had seen the deer lying down. There we found it a few yards from where it had been. I quickly looked at the antlers, and there in front of me was the seven-point buck. I stared at the buck in awe. Tim and I thanked God for the deer, and as we were dragging it to the house, we talked about the Kingdom and what we had just seen.

Yes, the Kingdom was that specific! No one ever told me that the Kingdom worked like this, that the Kingdom was that specific, and that we actually had that kind of authority.

Another Discovery

I can remember another deer hunt where I had planted my seed for a button buck. A button buck is a yearling buck, which has very small horns. Because they are so small, at a distance, the button buck can look like a doe. Because of this, button bucks count as does in the state of Ohio. Please note, they are not baby deer. They are not quite as big as a full-grown deer, but almost.

So on this particular day, I was up in my tree stand, and a whole group of deer came in, about nine or ten. They were slightly out of range of my bow but were slowly moving toward me. Suddenly, the neighbor cranked up their four-wheeler. At the sound, the whole herd took off running straight away from me. I said out loud, "Button buck, I command you to come back and stand under my tree." So get this picture. It is a harvested cornfield, and all nine deer are running straight away from me. At my word, a deer leaves the herd, continues running in a circle back around, comes directly under my tree stand, and stops! I took that deer home, and yes, it was a button buck.

This is the kind of thing I kept seeing over and over. I will discuss more about how incredibly detailed and specific the Kingdom is later in this book, but for now, let's just realize that something incredible is going on here.

The Kingdom changed our lives, and we could not stop telling people about it. We have so many stories, and we have seen so much. We have seen the dead come back to life, tumors instantly disappear, amazing financial stories, and amazing stories of deliverance and direction. With a hunger to tell people about the goodness of God's Kingdom, Drenda and I felt led to start Faith Life Church in 1995 to help people understand the Kingdom. God then directed us to launch Faith Life Now, our media ministry, in 2006, which broadcasts our TV ministry into every time zone on the planet on a daily basis. We found out that people everywhere want to know how to live this Kingdom lifestyle of freedom and victory.

God's Kingdom Works for Everyone

As I sat down to write this chapter this morning, I checked my emails. We get emails every day from people telling us how the Kingdom of God is changing their lives as well. I thought I would let you be part of my day as this email just came in a few minutes ago.

> Who am I that He is mindful of me? A few years ago, I started listening to your teachings, and I have seen miracles since. I have seen healings and financial miracles. Right now, my mind is truly blown as I look around and see His goodness. I see people in need and doors opened to the Gospel and truth. I see doors opened to the truth! And what blows me away is that I see my coffers full. He has enriched me so that I can give, so that others can see Him! I am a self-employed home inspector. I regularly mentor younger inspectors, and I started a Christians' business group where we talk about the call to be generous and to raise the next generation... that the Kingdom

way isn't competition but abundance. Seriously, your teaching has changed my life, and now it's being passed down to others; and as He has established me, others now listen and see His glory. It is so humbling to see what He's done and how He continues to provide. Thank you for your ministry!

Humbly,

B.F.

Knoxville, TN

This is the kind of email we get all the time. But we also get a lot of questions about the function of the Kingdom. People ask how to operate in the Kingdom and how to see the things that Drenda and I have seen. That is the purpose of this book, the fourth in my "Your Financial Revolution" series. If you have my other books, then you know I took some time up to this point to review some of the key concepts that anyone wanting to operate in the Kingdom needs to know.

But now I want to dig a bit deeper into the function of the Kingdom and, hopefully, help you understand more about how to live in the Kingdom with results. I want to start by laying out what I call the five basic steps to receive the provision you need from the Kingdom of God, just as God taught me.

The 5 Basic Steps to Receive the Provision You Need

Let's start with a story in Mark 8:14–21.

The disciples had forgotten to bring bread, except for one loaf they had with them in the boat. "Be careful," Jesus warned them. "Watch out for the yeast of the Pharisees and that of Herod."

They discussed this with one another and said, "It is because we have no bread."

*Aware of their discussion, Jesus asked them: "**Why are you talking about having no bread**? Do you still not see or understand? Are your hearts hardened? Do you have eyes but fail to see, and ears but fail to hear? And **don't you remember**? When I broke the five loaves for the five thousand, how many basketfuls of pieces did you pick up?"*

"Twelve," they replied.

"And when I broke the seven loaves for the four thousand, how many basketfuls of pieces did you pick up?"

They answered, "Seven."

He said to them, "Do you still not understand?"

—Mark 8:14-21

Basically, Jesus was saying, "Hey, guys, don't you remember? We have already covered this, and you already saw how we handled the shortage of bread in the past." But the disciples just could not wrap their heads around this. So Jesus told them to think back on what happened in the past. He was giving them a serious clue. "Think back to the last time we dealt with this same situation, and there you will find the answer." I would suggest that this is our answer as well. Yes, we see that the bread and fish multiplied, anyone can see that, but as spiritual scientists, we want to look deeper. How did it happen? So let's go back to the stories Jesus was referencing and look for clues.

By this time it was late in the day, so his disciples came to him. "This is a remote place," they said, "and it's already very late. Send the people away so that they can go to the surrounding countryside and villages and buy themselves something to eat."

But he answered, "You give them something to eat." They said to him, "That would take more than half a year's wages! Are we to go and spend that much on bread and give it to them to eat?"

"How many loaves do you have?" he asked. "Go and see." When they found out, they said, "Five—and two fish."

Then Jesus directed them to have all the people sit down in groups on the green grass. So they sat down in groups of hundreds and fifties. Taking the five loaves and the two fish and looking up to heaven, he gave thanks and broke the loaves. Then he gave them to his disciples to distribute to the people. He also divided the two fish among them all. They all ate and were satisfied, and the disciples picked up twelve basketfuls of broken pieces of bread and fish. The number of the men who had eaten was five thousand.
—Mark 6:35-44

I am sure that the disciples were shocked when upon asking Jesus about sending the people away to find food, He turned it back on them and said, "You feed them." "Them" in this case was actually more than 5,000 people. The Bible says there were 5,000 men there, so I can assume that there were women and children there as well, bringing the actual number to 15,000 to 20,000 people. I think anyone would agree that is a lot of people to feed, especially without any fair warning or preparation made beforehand.

Of course, I believe that Jesus was interested in feeding the people, but I think He was probably more intent on training His disciples in this situation than anything else. I believe this is why He told them, "You feed them." They had watched Jesus do many miracles, but now it was their turn. After all, He was going to be leaving in the near future, and Jesus wanted to be sure they would know how to handle life from a different perspective, the Kingdom's perspective.

> ## JESUS WANTED TO BE SURE THEY WOULD KNOW HOW TO HANDLE LIFE FROM A DIFFERENT PERSPECTIVE, THE KINGDOM'S PERSPECTIVE.

Step #1: What Do You Have?

"How many loaves do you have?" he asked. "Go and see."

When they found out, they said, "Five—and two fish."

Here is a major key. Jesus did not say, "Let's turn the rocks into bread." That would be spiritually illegal. Instead, He asked them what they already had. Specifically, He was asking how much of what they needed did they already have. He knew there was not enough bread and fish there to feed that crowd, and that was not the intent of His inquiry. Now, to the natural mind, the whole prospect of feeding those people sounded nuts. The disciples knew, without looking, that there was not going to be enough food to feed 20,000 people anywhere they looked. Can you imagine what they were thinking when Jesus told them to go and see how much bread and fish there actually was? And then to come back with their report that all they could find was five loaves of bread and two fish? Crazy, right?

Let me put this conversation into perspective. As a pastor, I have helped families in tough financial circumstances in the past, maybe by helping them pay a month's mortgage or rent payment, pay a few utility bills, or buy some groceries. But let's assume I knew the real answer was not giving them a handout, but instead, I knew the answer was the Kingdom.

The conversation would have gone something like this. "Hey, Pastor Gary, we ran really short this month, and we are getting close to being evicted from our home. Can the church help us out?" "Sure, I can help you. Here is my advice. Just pay the home off, and you will not have any payments to worry about." They would look at me and say, "Pastor, I do not think you understand. We do not have the money to pay the next house payment, let alone pay it off." "I know," I respond, "that is why I told you to pay off the house so you would not have any house payments."

And then if I asked them to go and see how much money they actually had that could be used toward paying off the house, they would really think I was nuts. But if out of obedience to me, they actually went and looked and came back and said, "We have double-checked, Pastor. All we could find was $20, but the balance on the mortgage is $360,000." I think you get the picture. They would think I had lost my mind, right?

This is how the disciples must have felt that day, totally confused. Five loaves and two fish to feed 20,000 people?

YOU REAP WHAT YOU SOW

Well, before we get deeper into this story, I need to sidetrack just for a moment to reveal another Kingdom law that is about to play out. Bread multiplies to bread, and fish multiplies to fish. So write this down.

YOU MUST RELEASE SOME OF WHAT YOU HAVE NEED OF INTO THE KINGDOM FOR IT TO MULTIPLY!

Let me jump to another example in the Bible, and then I will come back to our story in Mark 6. Let's go to 2 Kings 4:1-7.

> *The wife of a man from the company of the prophets cried out to Elisha, "Your servant my husband is dead, and you know that he revered the Lord. But now his creditor is coming to take my two boys as his slaves."*
>
> *Elisha replied to her, "**How can I help you? Tell me, what do you have in your house?**"*
>
> *"Your servant has nothing there at all," she said, "except a small jar of olive oil."*
>
> *Elisha said, "Go around and ask all your neighbors for empty jars. Don't ask for just a few. Then go inside and shut the door behind you and your sons. Pour oil into all the jars, and as each is filled, put it to one side."*
>
> *She left him and shut the door behind her and her sons. They brought the jars to her and she kept pouring. When all the jars*

were full, she said to her son, "Bring me another one."

But he replied, "There is not a jar left." Then the oil stopped flowing.

She went and told the man of God, and he said, "Go, sell the oil and pay your debts. You and your sons can live on what is left."
—2 Kings 4:1-7

Notice the prophet did not say, "Well, let's go over to the treasury and see what we have." No, he knew of a better way to solve this. He said, "How can I help you?" The woman may have been slightly confused as she responded, "How can you help me? I need money!" But he was not trying to belittle her. He was asking a very important question that he knew would lead to her answer. It is the same question that will lead to your answer as well.

<u>How can I help you? Tell me, what do you have in your house?</u>

What Do You Have?

What do you have in your house? I am sure she was a bit shocked at the question because she had already explained why she was there.

"Your servant has nothing there at all," she said, "except a small jar of olive oil."

Notice her emphasis, "nothing there at all." But did she really have nothing?

No, her statement was not technically correct. She did say that she had a small jar of olive oil. Bingo! That is all the prophet was waiting to find out.

And that is all you need to ask yourself as well. God just needs something that is under your legal jurisdiction to work with.

So let's review the first step. You will need to give God some of what you have need of. When you give it to the Kingdom of God, it changes jurisdiction, putting it under God's legal dominion so that it can multiply. Let's remember that to multiply may not mean what we saw in this story, that your bread will actually just multiply all by itself as it sits in your cupboard, although I have seen that type of thing happen. But usually, God will make a way for the bread to multiply through an interaction with other people. Someone might be generous toward you, or you get that raise at work, or an unexpected refund may show up. There are countless ways that God can multiply your bread back to you.

WHEN YOU GIVE IT TO THE KINGDOM OF GOD, IT CHANGES JURISDICTION, PUTTING IT UNDER GOD'S LEGAL DOMINION SO THAT IT CAN MULTIPLY.

You Can Name Your Money

I want to point out a very important point about money.

Money can be used as a seed for anything.

You name money every day of your life whenever you buy something. For instance, when you are at the grocery store and you buy bread, you are exchanging your money for that bread, or in reality, you are naming your money "bread." Let's examine what I mean. If you need bread, you now understand a law of the Kingdom called sowing and reaping. By applying that law, you know that if you sow bread, you will get bread. But let's assume that you need bread, but you do not have bread to sow. What would you do? You could sow money and name it bread as you sow it. Remember, money is simply a bartering system. We name it every day for everything we need from milk and rent to shoes and food. So you can name money when you give it also.

You can name your money when you give it.

Faith Life Church, in New Albany, Ohio, is the church that Drenda and I started over 25 years ago. We built the Now Center, the campus where Faith Life Church is located in 2008. It was a formidable project running 6.5 million dollars at the time, a large project for about 550 people to undertake.

Well, over the last 10 years, we have maxed out that building. Running around 3,000 on the weekends is just about all we can do. Running four live services every weekend is really all I can do. So we decided to add on to our current building. It was going to be a 10-million dollar project and would enable us to grow by increasing the size of our auditorium and adding children's space. At the same time, we realized that the time needed to raise the money and then the time needed to actually build the building would be an issue. It meant we would be looking at a two and a half year waiting period to actually be able to use the added space.

With that in mind, we felt we should go ahead and move forward with adding on to our building but at the same time begin to look at a campus site, which we felt we could have up and running in about six months. We believed this would take some of the pressure off the main campus while at the same time allow the church to grow. So we put a team together to begin the search for a campus site. We studied our demographics and settled on an area of town that we felt would be a great location in our city. We looked and looked and almost pulled the trigger a couple of times on several different locations, but when we sat down to actually agree that this was the site, we all would agree that something still was not right. We all felt a check in our spirits.

Now let's fast forward six months, and we find ourselves nowhere closer to finding our new campus site than we were on day one. I will have to admit, Drenda and I were tempted to get a little discouraged in the search. We had looked at every available option in our search area and still were not finding a building that would really be ideal. Yes, we had sown our seed at the beginning of the journey, and we knew that God had the perfect building for us, but we had not expected it to take this long to materialize. Here is a hint: perfect sometimes takes longer!

At this time, we were scheduled to be a part of a fundraising telethon to raise money for a new TV network. This would be a three-day event which would be live and on the air in the mornings and the evenings all three days. I think it was the third day, and I was just sitting on the set when I heard the Lord speak to me. He said, "Take a $100,000 check from the ministry and sow that into this TV outreach with the intent of breaking this campus stalemate. Take the check to each of your four services, and have the church pray over that gift as you release it, calling the campus location finished!" He went on to say that when I prayed to rebuke Satan and command the confusion and delay to stop. Well, we did that the next weekend in our Saturday and Sunday services.

The next day, which was Monday, my campus team said that the real estate agent had called, and he had just found out about a private high school campus that was just placed on the market. They decided to take a look at it. When they went to look, they found a complete K–12 campus, including a preschool. It was listed for much more than we were wanting to spend on a campus as, in reality, we were looking to lease our new site to conserve cash flow for the main campus addition. Although the price was not really something we could consider, Drenda and I decided to take a look at it on Tuesday morning.

What we saw was an amazing campus site with 88,000 square feet, four buildings, a running track, weight room, four tennis courts, a dedicated arts building, science labs, and basically everything that a K-12 school campus would need. The incredible part of the story is that it was completely furnished and stocked with supplies. Drenda and I were in awe but could see no way to actually purchase the property.

It just so happened that we had an appointment that night with one of our partners just to get together and to catch up with each other. We had rescheduled this dinner appointment probably three or four times over the last two months due to both of us being so busy. But that night, we made it. As we were sitting there at supper, we began to talk about the addition to the main church. The couple asked us about how fast things were moving, and we told them about some major delays in permits and blueprints and other issues we were having. We told them it looked like we would not get into the addition until the end of 2022 or the spring of 2023 at the pace things were moving.

They immediately asked if we had ever thought of launching a campus, and we said yes. We explained how we had been searching for the last six months without finding a suitable site. We then told them of the awesome school we had just looked at that morning, saying that something like that would be perfect, but it was on the market for millions.

The couple sat there and did not bat an eye but simply said,

"Well, what if it was free?" We really did not catch on right away, and they asked again, "What if it was free?" Again, we thought they were kidding, but this time the gentleman said, "Drenda, what if the campus was free?" "What do you mean?" we asked. They said, "We will write the check!" We were stunned for a moment as we sat there. But to make a long story short, they did.

So two days after we sowed that seed for our campus, God directed us to the perfect site. We now own a 12-million dollar campus free and clear! Who would have ever thought or, quite frankly, even imagined that? After we saw that, Drenda and I both agreed that even with all we have seen, we need to think bigger. God can do some pretty awesome things!

I guess it must have felt the same to the disciples that day after feeding 20,000 people with five loaves and two fish. I bet they went to bed saying, "Wow, did you see that?"

CHAPTER 5
EMPOWERING YOUR PROVISION

We talked in the last chapter about the first step in engaging Kingdom law for your provision.

YOU MUST RELEASE SOME OF WHAT YOU HAVE NEED OF INTO THE KINGDOM FOR IT TO MULTIPLY!

I told you then that I would answer a couple of questions regarding this statement, the first being, "What does it mean to release something into the Kingdom for it to multiply?"

Again, let's go back to our story in Mark 6 for some insight.

> *By this time it was late in the day, so his disciples came to him. "This is a remote place," they said, "and it's already very late. Send the people away so that they can go to the surrounding countryside and villages and buy themselves something to eat."*
>
> *But he answered, "You give them something to eat." They said to him, "That would take more than half a year's wages! Are we to go and spend that much on bread and give it to them to eat?"*
>
> *"How many loaves do you have?" he asked. "Go and see." When they found out, they said, "Five—and two fish."*

Then Jesus directed them to have all the people sit down in groups on the green grass. So they sat down in groups of hundreds and fifties. Taking the five loaves and the two fish and looking up to heaven, he gave thanks and broke the loaves. Then he gave them to his disciples to distribute to the people. He also divided the two fish among them all. They all ate and were satisfied, and the disciples picked up twelve basketfuls of broken pieces of bread and fish. The number of the men who had eaten was five thousand.

—Mark 6:35-44

I want you to notice a few things in that story that you may overlook. When Jesus said, "You give them something to eat," their answer and His response show us one of the most important keys to our understanding of the Kingdom in regard to provision. When they answered Him, they said it would take more than half a year's wages to feed that many people. Notice how their minds tied their needed provision to labor when faced with that problem. Well, the fact is we all do that. But this dollars for hours mentality was not always part of man's consciousness. It came about at the Fall with Adam. I need to take you back to Adam's fall where we can clearly see this take place.

The Dollars for Hours Mentality

To Adam he said, "Because you listened to your wife and ate fruit from the tree about which I commanded you, 'You must not eat from it,' cursed is the ground because of you; through painful toil you will eat food from it all the days of your life. It will produce thorns and thistles for you, and you will eat the plants of

the field. By the sweat of your brow you will eat your food until you return to the ground, since from it you were taken; for dust you are and to dust you will return."
—Genesis 3:17-19

If you remember, Adam and Eve were placed on the earth to rule over it on behalf of the Kingdom of God. They ruled with delegated authority. Satan, already on the earth, despised them and lusted after the authority they had. Although Adam and Eve had complete authority over him, he managed to deceive them into believing that God was not for them and was untrustworthy. He offered them what appeared to be a better future, so they decided to follow him instead of God. Because of their rebellion, they lost their legal positions in the Kingdom of God and essentially kicked God out of their lives, giving Satan legal jurisdiction over the entire earth realm as it pertains to mankind. Paul calls Satan the god of this age here in 2 Corinthians.

The god of this age has blinded the minds of unbelievers, so that they cannot see the light of the gospel that displays the glory of Christ, who is the image of God.
—2 Corinthians 4:4

Being confronted with his sin, God says to Adam, "Cursed is the ground because of you; through painful toil you will eat your food all the days of your life." Then dropping down a sentence, it says, "By the sweat of your brow you will eat your food."

God is telling Adam that because of his rebellion, the earth will not produce like it had in the past. God's hands are now tied, and Adam will have to make his own way through life by his own sweat and painful labor. Please note that Adam is the one who cursed the earth, not God. Adam had complete legal jurisdiction over the earth, and when he rebelled against God, the blessing of God was forced to withdraw. This is why God says to Adam, "**Cursed is the ground because of you**." The Garden where Adam was created to live, which was full of provision, was gone. Previous to his rebellion, Adam would never have had a thought or concern about provision; it was abundantly supplied everywhere he looked. But now he would have to find his own provision through his own painful toil and sweat. I call this the painful toil and sweat system.

Painful toil and sweat were now required to produce provision!

The earth is not the only thing that changed. Adam and all mankind have now changed. Adam has lost his identity, his purpose, and his provision and has now become a slave to survival. This is how you and I grew up as well, under the painful toil and sweat system.

Every decision under this earth curse system is one of survival, and is usually based around finding money or dealing with money issues. Where and how to find the provision we need rules our thoughts and our lives. Our identities, which once were uniquely designed by God for our purposes and assignments on the earth

SINCE ADAM'S TIME, MEN AND WOMEN HAVE BEEN ENSLAVED TO SURVIVAL, EITHER RUNNING AFTER PROVISION OR HOARDING PROVISION, BECAUSE HAVING MONEY IS THE ONLY ESCAPE FROM THE RAT RACE.

have now been hijacked and replaced by our need to find the money we need to survive, always looking for the next day's provision.

A System of Slavery

A recent survey I spotted said that over 70% of the people in the United States do not like their jobs.[5] You might ask, "Then why do they go to work if they do not like it?" Simply put, they are slaves to the next paycheck!

Under the earth curse of painful toil and sweat, everyone dreams of being a millionaire, of an escape from the endless rat race and pressure to find provision. People dream of winning the lottery, dream of being rich where they would be free to do what they want to do instead what they have to do. Since Adam's time, men and women have been enslaved to survival, either running after provision or hoarding provision, because having money is the only escape from the rat race.

Let me give you an example of how this system has trained all of us how to think. If I told you that you had to get completely out of debt over the next 12 months, you would automatically begin to calculate how to exert more painful toil and sweat into the equation to get it done. You would calculate how you could work two or three jobs, if needed, whatever it took. And what it took was more painful toil and sweat. Painful toil and sweat is the denominator that is factored into every dream. If you need a new car, you would divide the cost by labor and sweat and say, "No, we cannot afford it." "A bigger house? No, we cannot afford it."

God Sees Possibilities in Impossibilities

Under the earth curse system, dreams are replaced by short trips

---

5 https://returntonow.net/2017/09/22/85-people-hate-jobs-gallup-poll-says

YOUR FINANCIAL REVOLUTION: The Power of Provision

to Walmart and then a burger on the way home. And if there was not enough time or labor to accomplish your dream, you abandoned it and admitted to yourself that you should just continue going to that job you hate like everyone else does. The painful toil and sweat equation usually has the word impossible after the equals sign for most people.

And this is exactly how the disciples perceived their situation, "Feed these 20,000 people? Impossible! That would take over six months' wages!" Wages in this case meant more painful toil and labor than was possible to meet the need. Again, their only perception of obtaining provision was through labor. This is the way it works in the earth realm. Everyone knows that, but Jesus is about to show them a new way of living, a new Kingdom with new laws. Yes, there really is an escape out of the painful toil and sweat system. There really is!

Let's go back to that moment when the disciples said it would be impossible to feed that crowd and watch how Jesus responds. You probably should have a DWJD (Do What Jesus Did) leather bracelet made so you will not forget what He is about to show us, like His disciples did. Instead of agreeing with His disciples' diagnosis of the situation, Jesus instead takes charge by giving them a directive, "Go and see how many loaves you have." Now, they knew before they even looked that there was not going to be enough for them to feed the entire crowd. This was why they came to Jesus in the first place and asked Him to send the people away to find food on their own. But out of obedience, they went and looked and came back with the report of locating a meager five loaves and two fish.

Now, something happens here that you must see, another major clue! But to see it, I want to look at the same story but in Matthew's version.

> Jesus replied, "They do not need to go away. You give them something to eat."

"We have here only five loaves of bread and two fish," they answered.

"<u>Bring them here to me</u>," he said. And he directed the people to sit down on the grass. Taking the five loaves and the two fish and looking up to heaven, he gave thanks and broke the loaves. Then he gave them to the disciples, and the disciples gave them to the people. They all ate and were satisfied, and the disciples picked up twelve basketfuls of broken pieces that were left over. The number of those who ate was about five thousand men, besides women and children.

—Matthew 14:16-21

Notice in verse 18 that Jesus asks the disciples to bring the bread and fish to Him. Then at the end of verse 19, we see that He gives the bread and fish back to His disciples. Something happened between those two segments of Scripture that should have caught your attention and prompted a question: "Why did Jesus ask the disciples to bring the bread and fish to Him if He was just going to give them right back to them in the next moment?" Jesus does not do anything religiously, so there must be a reason He asked for the bread and fish. As spiritual scientists, we need to know what happened when He took the bread and fish from the disciples.

Taking the five loaves and the two fish and looking up to heaven, he gave thanks and broke the loaves. Then he gave them to the disciples, and the disciples gave them to the people.

The Bible says He gave thanks. Some versions say He blessed it.

But what does that mean? The Greek word used here for thanks or blessing literally means to consecrate a thing, to ask God's blessing on a thing, or to ask God to bless something for one's use. Taking that a step further, to consecrate something means to declare it as sacred, dedicated formally to a divine purpose.

So basically, when Jesus blessed the fish and bread, they were separated from the earth realm's jurisdiction to heaven's jurisdiction. **When He spoke over them and blessed them, the bread and fish changed kingdoms.**

Bringing Things Under a New Jurisdiction

The bread and fish were previously under the jurisdiction of men in the earth realm and outside of God's ability to do something with them. But now we see that through the generosity of the little boy, they have been offered to Jesus, where they are transferred under the Kingdom's jurisdiction. We must also realize that left under the jurisdiction of the earth realm, the bread and fish could never have multiplied.

As spiritual scientists, we need to pay close attention to the details. When did this transfer actually happen? You may at first think that the change in jurisdiction occurred when the little boy gave the fish and bread to the disciples. That was, of course, part of the process, and that the boy did it willingly is also an important clue to factor in. But giving the bread and fish to the disciples was not where the actual transfer occurred. It was the moment that Jesus spoke over it, when He blessed it, that the actual legal transfer occurred. I submit that even though Jesus had taken possession of the bread and fish and was holding them in His hands, they would not have multiplied until He spoke over them with a specific directive.

Let's put that in perspective to our faith lesson we learned earlier. We found out that even though your heart can be in faith, which now makes it legal for heaven to invade Earth, nothing happens until you, having legal jurisdiction on the earth, release heaven's authority here.

> *For it is with your heart that you believe and are justified, and it is with your mouth that you profess your faith and are saved.*
> —Romans 10:10

Although Jesus's words are not recorded in the Bible here in regard to what He said when He blessed the bread and the fish, I am sure they may have gone something like this: "Father, I thank you for your provision, and I receive this bread and fish into your Kingdom for your glory. This bread and fish shall now multiply so that they may feed this massive crowd with more than enough, so they may find rest and strength and see your glory." Of course, as I said, His words are not recorded. But I am sure He gave the bread and fish a directive after they were placed in His hands. How do I know that? Because He already knew what the plan was and already had them sitting in groups.

> *Jesus replied, "They do not need to go away. You give them something to eat."*
>
> *"We have here only five loaves of bread and two fish," they answered.*
>
> *"Bring them here to me," he said. And he directed the people to sit down on the grass. Taking the five loaves and the two fish and looking up to heaven, he gave thanks and broke the loaves. Then*

he gave them to the disciples, and the disciples gave them to the people.

—Matthew 14:16-19

Notice that He had already given them instructions to sit down in the grass before He blessed the bread and fish. He knew exactly what His plan was. I am sure He gave the bread and fish a directive after they were placed in His hands. Giving a directive when you release your seed is a vital aspect of releasing your seed. Did I say vital? I did, so pay attention. I need to spend some time right here in regard to giving a directive when you sow.

"But what about you?" he asked. "Who do you say I am?"

Simon Peter answered, "You are the Messiah, the Son of the living God."

Jesus replied, "Blessed are you, Simon son of Jonah, for this was not revealed to you by flesh and blood, but by my Father in heaven. And I tell you that you are Peter, and on this rock I will build my church, and the gates of Hades will not overcome it. <u>I will give you the keys of the kingdom of heaven; whatever you bind on earth will be bound in heaven, and whatever you loose on earth will be loosed in heaven</u>."

—Matthew 16:15-19

This Scripture clearly tells us that our ability to rule on the earth on behalf of the Kingdom of God has now been restored through Jesus Christ. We have been given authority to bind the devil and loose heaven's will into the earth. Now, I believe, or at least I hope, that many Christians already know what binding the devil means. Very simply, binding the devil means stopping him from carrying out his wicked plans. That can occur by you casting demons out of people, laying your hands on the sick and them recovering, or simply by saying, "Stop, in the name of Jesus!" You are taking your authority in the Kingdom of God and using it to enforce the victory that Jesus won over the devil.

> **WE HAVE BEEN GIVEN AUTHORITY TO BIND THE DEVIL AND LOOSE HEAVEN'S WILL INTO THE EARTH.**

Using Your Authority

In my observation, very few people know how to loose heaven into the earth realm. I have already talked about 1 John 5:14-15 as an outline for effective prayer.

> *This is the confidence we have in approaching God: that if we ask anything according to his will, he hears us. And if we know that he hears us—whatever we ask—we know that we have what we asked of him.*
>
> —1 John 5:14 -15

Believing in your heart or having faith is not the end of the equation. As we have already seen, when you believe what heaven says, you are justified. It is now legal for heaven to flow into the earth realm, but nothing happens until you release that authority into the earth realm. You are seated with Christ in heavenly places on the right hand of the Father. Your words are the words of a king, and heaven cannot be released here until you speak! This can be a declaration or an agreement spoken in prayer, but you hold the keys of the Kingdom. God cannot do it without you!

It is not just a matter of knowing how to go through the action of praying that makes things happen; it is knowing to give a directive when you do so. Remember, if you do not loose heaven here in the earth, it will not be done. So it is imperative that we understand how to loose heaven's will into our lives and our world.

One of the best examples of giving a directive is taught in the Lord's Prayer. There are some major keys here in the Lord's Prayer you need to be aware of. First, the text says that God already knows what you need, so stop the begging. Begging is not faith, and it shows ignorance relative to how the Kingdom works and your rights as a citizen of the Kingdom. Giving a directive in prayer is really making a requisition. A requisition is a very detailed list of what you need. It is not asking for those items; it is laying claim to those items.

> *And when you pray, do not keep on babbling like pagans, for they think they will be heard because of their many words. Do not be like them, for your Father knows what you need before you ask him. This, then, is how you should pray: "Our Father in heaven, hallowed be your name, your kingdom come, your will be done, on earth as it is in heaven. Give us today our daily bread."*
>
> —Matthew 6:7-11

Jesus starts off with, "Our Father in heaven, hallowed (greatly revered and honored) be your name (reflecting on His dominion and authority)." Jesus is setting the legal posture of prayer in this first sentence. Let's compare it to the first sentence spoken in a courtroom.

A bailiff stands and says, "Please rise. The court of (then he names the court)...." It could be the Common Pleas Court of Franklin County or the Second Judicial Circuit Court, Criminal Division, or any other name. But several things happen there in the beginning. The bailiff says, "All rise," setting the honor due to the court as well as to the judge who will be presiding over the court. The name of the court is mentioned to establish proper jurisdiction, so that you know you are in the right courtroom which has jurisdiction over your case.

Let's go on with what the bailiff says. "Please rise. The Common Pleas Court of Franklin County is now is session, the Honorable Judge Smith presiding."

This whole first sentence, "**Our Father in heaven, hallowed be your name**," is setting the posture of the One who is to rule this case and authorizes us to be there. He is our Father, and we have legal access to this court. This first sentence also locates the jurisdiction of the court as being heaven's court, the highest court of all authority.

Next, the Lord's Prayer says, "**Your kingdom come, your will be done.**"

This phrase is putting a demand on the court to rule according to the law of the Kingdom. You are about to make a request or bring an issue to the court, and you are asking the Judge to enforce what His will (the law) says in regard to this case. Next it says, "**On earth as it is in heaven**." Again, you are stating that you want this ruling in heaven to be enforced on Earth as it is in heaven. Now, all of this was to establish and posture you and the court. Nothing has been asked or presented yet. But next comes the petition.

"Give us this day our daily bread." This statement really does not have much to do with bread unless that is exactly what you need. Instead, it is telling you to insert what it is you need. Remember, this whole conversation began where Jesus was instructing His disciples how to pray to get their needs met. This is where you make your petition, but as I said, a better word to be used here is requisition.

BUT MOST CHRISTIANS WOULD SAY SOMETHING LIKE THIS, "OH, WHATEVER GOD WANTS TO BRING ME IS FINE. HE KNOWS BEST." WRONG, WRONG, WRONG!

Of course, both will work, and petition is what Philippians 4 says. But the point I want to get across is a petition is a detailed request. The point to remember is detailed. You are giving a directive in prayer; it has to be detailed and exact. Philippians 4:6-7 tell us the same thing.

> *Do not be anxious about anything, but in every situation, by prayer and petition, with thanksgiving, present your requests to God. And the peace of God, which transcends all understanding, will guard your hearts and your minds in Christ Jesus.*
> —Philippians 4:6-7

Notice that prayers and petitions are different. Our prayers carry our petitions, but prayers are the vehicles that take them to our Father. Again, a petition is very detailed and precise. But most Christians would say something like this, "Oh, whatever God wants to bring me is fine. He knows best." Wrong, Wrong, Wrong!

God has given YOU the keys of the Kingdom!

If you have read much of my material, you would have seen countless detailed stories of the Kingdom. There are many in this book that I hope will help you see just how detailed the Kingdom is and just how detailed your words need to be. To make my point, let me possibly bore you with a couple of older stories that you may have heard before. But I feel I need to spend as much time as needed for you to have a good understanding of just how specific the Kingdom is. Let me just run through a few reminders of stories we have talked about.

The Kingdom at Work

You read previously how my van burned up after I said out loud, "Lord, it might be best if this van just burned up." Coincidence? Let's move on. I told you about the deer, how the Lord showed me to sow for them, and how I have never had a deer come under my tree stand that I did not sow for. The right deer, the deer that I sowed for, came every single time. Then I showed you how God showed me that the deer were coming in the order that I sowed for them. Come on; have you ever heard something like that before? I know I never have until I saw it with my own eyes. The Kingdom is so exact that I told you about the seven-point experiment and the six-point that Tim sowed for. I told you how God taught me to speak with authority, and the buck that was walking away from me at 200 yards stopped the second I spoke, then came and stood directly beneath my tree stand. I told you about the pheasant where I commanded it to stop, and it instantly stopped in its tracks.

I told you about the gun I pointed to in the sporting goods store while I said, "I will take that one," and a few weeks later, I was given that exact gun. I also told you about the BMW 645Ci convertible that Drenda saw across the parking lot and said, "That's it!" We told no one, but a couple of weeks later, a man in the church called me and said, "I saw Drenda's car today." I was shocked and asked him what he meant. He went on to say that as he was driving through town, he saw a BMW 645Ci convertible in perfect shape for sale; and as he saw it, the Lord told him it was Drenda's car. That caught my attention, the exact car!

I am going to tell you a story in chapter 7 of how I received the exact plane I had sown for from a totally unexpected source and how I got the money to pay for it. I have countless stories that demonstrate how exact the Kingdom works.

I remember when I shot my big 26-point buck. It was a fairly warm day for November. I let the deer hang all that day, and the next day I took it to the taxidermist to have its head mounted. He looked at the fur and said, "I am sorry; it looks like the warm weather has ruined the fur. I do not think this is going to work, but I will try it and see." Now, I was not about to let the trophy buck that I had harvested by faith fail to make a great mount for my office. At that moment, he went into the office to grab an order form. When he walked in the office, I laid my hand on the buck and declared that the fur was perfect and the mount would turn out perfectly. Well, I went back in a month to get the mount, and the taxidermist said, "You know, I told you I thought the fur was ruined, but this mount turned out perfect. The fur is perfect."

I could go on for hours like this, but the bottom line is what are you saying? With every word, you are setting in motion spiritual law! You might not have known that. I know I didn't, but it is true. The Kingdom is very specific. Let me tell you one more story, and you will see many more stories throughout the remainder of this book that will prove what I am saying. As you can tell, I am passionate about getting this across.

Setting Spiritual Law in Motion

It was during one of Drenda's women's conferences. We had rented a Cadillac Escalade to drive a guest around while she was in town. At the end of the conference, the Escalade did not have to be back until the morning, so Drenda and I decided to drive it home that night to see how it drove. We had never driven an Escalade before. Well, as you can imagine, it drove great. As we drove it back to church the next morning, we were talking, and we agreed that we would like to have one. The one we drove was a short version and was in pearl white. We both agreed that we liked the short version better than the longer version, and we loved the pearl white.

Well, it was only a month or so after that event that as I was stepping outside to get my paper, the cell phone rang, and the voice on the other end was one of my church members. He simply said, "I would like to buy you a Cadillac Escalade. What color would you like?" I was taken off guard but said a pearl white one. I forgot to mention the short version, however. Well, about a month went by, and I thought that possibly he had forgotten about the Escalade, but the phone rang, and he said that he had one. So we went to meet him, and he had a perfect pearl white short version Escalade. As we walked up to it, he said the following, "I am sorry that it took so long, but I couldn't find a long one." What he did not know was that we did not want the long one. He liked the long one and thought that is the one we would want, but the short one is the only one he could find. Again, the perfect, exact vehicle we had spoken out in agreement.

An amazing example that I saw in business happened over the last few years. As you may or may not know, I still own a financial services company. Before I started pastoring 25 years ago, I had the number one office out of 5,000 offices for one of my vendors. When I launched my church, I knew that I would be very busy and assumed that I would not be able to maintain that number one position, which I did not. In my business, our vendors offer incentive trips to reward their salespeople for that year's production.

One vendor that I used gave their top ten offices $100,000 in bonuses at their annual convention for anyone that did over $10 million in volume. They also paid for a very nice trip to the annual convention for anyone who did over $3 million. I usually did about $4 million every year with this company, so I would get the free trip, and then I would have to sit there and watch them give out the $100,000 checks to the top ten every year. I did this for 18 years! That's right, for 18 years. I never thought I could reach that goal while pastoring the church, so I never set my faith in that direction.

But one year as I was sitting at the convention watching the top ten get their $100,000 checks, the Lord spoke to me and said, "Why are you not up there?" Before I could answer, He said, "I want you up there. I want My name to be seen here." Well, it was already March, and like I said, we had been doing about $4 million a year for the last 18 years for this company. In the natural, I did not see any way to make that goal, but I prayed about it, and Drenda and I sowed our seed to reach that $10 million mark. The Lord showed me a change I could make in regard to how my company processed inquiries, which made a big difference. Well, to make a long story short, we made the top ten and got that $100,000 check. But here is the part I want to share with you. We made it by one sale!

The next year, the company raised the goal to $12 million to reach the $100,000 check level. So we sowed our seed, and we made it that year as well. But you guessed it; we made it by one sale. The next two years, the program was cancelled. But last year, in 2019, they started it up again at the $10 million level. We sowed our seed and made it to the top ten; and you guessed it. Again, we made it by one sale. Was it a coincidence that we made it every year by one sale? No, we were sowing to reach the minimum number to get into that $100,000 check level. And that is exactly what we did. Did we mean to make it by only one case? Of course not. We were going at it full speed all year long and did not know where things were going to fall until the last day of the month. Again, an amazing picture of just how this thing works.

The Importance of Giving a Directive

At this year's Provision Conference, God spoke to me and told me to teach people what Drenda and I had learned about giving a directive. This is exactly what the Holy Spirit called it, a directive. So I did spend some time teaching along this line as I know so many people do not know much about doing this. According to the dictionary, a directive is an official or authoritative instruction. Notice it did not say a begging for mercy, woe is me instruction. No, it is an authoritative instruction! So let's take this a step further. If I am giving a directive spiritually, who carries it out? Yes, someone does; let's find out who.

> *"Have faith in God," Jesus answered. "Truly I tell you, if anyone says to this mountain, 'Go, throw yourself into the sea,' and does not doubt in their heart but believes that what they say will happen, it will be done for them. Therefore I tell you, whatever you ask for in prayer, believe that you have received it, and it will be yours."*
>
> —Mark 11:22-24

There are two things in this passage that I want to point out. Notice that it says, "If anyone says." Here we see what Drenda and I had discovered. Our words release heaven here in the earth realm. Secondly, I want to focus on this portion of that passage.

> *"...and does not doubt in their heart but believes that*
> *what they say will happen, it <u>will be done for them</u>."*

Notice it says, "It will be done for them!" Not for God, but for them, the ones that are speaking here on the earth.

Wow! Stop everything. You need to think on that for a minute! Let it sink in; this is talking about you.

So who does it for them? Let's look at Hebrews 1:14 to find out.

> *Are not all angels <u>ministering</u> spirits sent to <u>serve</u> those who will*
> *inherit salvation?*

Notice there are two different words describing angels here, minister and serve. To serve means to perform duties or services for another person, in this case for you. Minister means a high officer of state entrusted with the management of a division of governmental activities. To paraphrase what an angel is, he is a representative of the court of heaven with authorization to act on behalf of the Kingdom of God on your behalf! Please note that we cannot boss angels around as they do not report to us, but we can petition the court of heaven for what we need, and they will be dispatched. Pretty incredible!

"I have to say something? I did not know that." This describes the lesson God taught me in the following story.

In this particular year, I had sown my seed for a button buck. At the time of this story, I was very confident of receiving my deer. So I went out expecting, as usual, that I would have my button buck in short order. As I sat in my tree stand, I did indeed see a button buck walking through the woods, but he was too far away for me to take a shot with my bow. I tried telling it to come to me, but nothing. I did not see anything else the whole morning. I went out the following morning and did not even see a deer. At this point, I knew something was very wrong.

As I was walking out of the woods on that second day, I began to pray in the Holy Spirit for the answer. Very quickly, the Holy Spirit showed me what was wrong. When I sowed for my deer, I had simply written out my seed check, put it in an envelope, and mailed it off. I did not lay my hands on that check and speak over it as I usually did. Then the Holy Spirit reminded me of the story where Jesus multiplied the bread and fish and pointed out that Jesus blessed it before it could multiply. I remember thinking, *I have to do that?* Now, I had always laid my hands on that envelope and spoken over it in the past, but I was really busy the day that I sent that envelope off that year and just forgot to. I thought that just sowing my seed was what brought the deer under the jurisdiction of the Kingdom.

Well, I was anxious to correct my error and try out my new understanding of the Kingdom to see if I was right. So I sowed my seed again for a button buck, but this time, I was sure to speak over it as I sowed it. When I say speak over it, let me give you an example of what I might say. "Father, today I receive a button buck, in the name of Jesus, as I sow this seed. I call it done according to Mark 11:24, and I thank you for it. Holy Spirit, bring that button buck in range for a perfect shot, in Jesus's name. Amen." As you can see, nothing fancy, but I am not asking or begging for the deer. I am declaring, making my petition known. Someone on the front lines in the military does not need to ask for ammunition; they simply put in a requisition. In other words, they already have legal access to whatever they need, no need to ask, just say, "Pass the ammunition."

Well, the next morning, I was out in my tree stand before light, and just as the woods began to turn grey, I saw a lone deer making its way toward me. It was too dark to shoot, but I could see the deer coming straight for my tree. As the deer approached my tree, it stopped, and over the next 15 minutes, it slowly walked around my tree. I was surprised, to say the least. The deer just stayed within 20 yards of my tree and just slowly circled it.

As the light in the woods slowly brightened, I could see that it was not a buck with antlers. In fact, it looked like a doe as I could not make out any buttons on the deer's head. It still was not totally light yet, but it was now legal to shoot as Ohio has a legal shooting time in the morning. I could not tell if it was a button buck, as I said, but I also knew that many times, the small button antlers are just below the fur. I figured that as strange as the deer had behaved, it had to be my deer, so I took the shot and dropped the deer. As I approached the deer, I was pleased to see the small buttons and realized that it was indeed my button buck. I left the buck lay where it fell as I realized I had forgotten to bring my knife with me, so I walked back up to the house to get one.

When I got back to the deer, I saw Tim walking toward me. He asked if I had seen anything, and I explained the events of the morning. As we walked over to where the button buck lay, he said that he had not even seen a deer in the last three days he had been out. Tim had gone with me all three days, and now as he said that, I knew what the problem was. I remembered the day that he came by my office and handed me a check for his deer seed, which he was sowing to the church. I remembered he did not speak over his seed either. I took some time and explained what God had shown me concerning speaking over the seed as it was being sown.

That night, Tim and I had some business to attend to in Columbus, and on the way home, we would be passing right by the church. Tim asked if he could stop and sow his seed again, this time speaking over it as he released it. As we sat in my office, he made out his seed, and on it I saw he was sowing for a six-point buck. I thought that was a rather bold and specific declaration.

Well, the next morning, Tim went to the same tree I had used the day before. He experienced the same thing I had the day before. Before light, a buck came directly to the tree and just walked in circles around it until shooting light. Tim took the shot and felt he had a pretty good hit on the buck. Unfortunately, the buck ran out of sight, and although we searched for two hours, we just could not locate it. Amazingly, later that day, a friend of ours, who lives about three-quarters of a mile from us, told us that his neighbor had gotten up that morning and found a six-point buck lying dead in his driveway. The buck had an arrow in it. This neighbor's house was the exact direction from our woods that the deer had run. My friend told us that his neighbor, not knowing who had shot the deer, butchered the deer himself that morning. Crazy story I know, but lesson learned.

Speak over your seed when you release it, just like Jesus did.

By the way, Tim sowed a new seed and went out and got his buck the next week.

When You Speak, Be Specific

I know that a six-point buck is pretty specific, but as we were finding out, the Kingdom is specific! Take a look at nature, for instance.

> *For since the creation of the world God's invisible qualities—his eternal power and divine nature—have been clearly seen, being understood from what has been made, so that people are without excuse.*

> —Romans 1:20

The Bible says that God's invisible qualities are seen in nature. So let me ask you a question, "How detailed is nature?" Extremely detailed! If I told you that I was going to buy a car, your next question to me would be, "What kind of car?" right? You cannot see a car in your mind when I say car. You see "the car" as a very specific car, a Ford or Chevy, a certain model car with a certain color. There is no picture with the word car: it is always a specific car. This is how you need to be in your prayer life as well.

Have you ever read a legal document? I am sure you have. They are extremely detailed. Well, what you release with your words is that exact as well, even when you do not want them to be. Watch how Jesus ministered. He understood the importance of words.

> *When Jesus came down from the mountainside, large crowds followed him. A man with leprosy came and knelt before him and said, "Lord, if you are willing, you can make me clean."*
>
> *Jesus reached out his hand and touched the man. "I am willing," he said. "Be clean!" Immediately he was cleansed of his leprosy.*
>
> —Matthew 8:1-3

Notice nothing happened until Jesus said, "Be clean!"

> *When he arrived at the other side in the region of the Gadarenes, two demon-possessed men coming from the tombs met him. They were so violent that no one could pass that way. "What do you want with us, Son of God?" they shouted. "Have you come here to torture us before the appointed time?"*
>
> *Some distance from them a large herd of pigs was feeding. The*

demons begged Jesus, "If you drive us out, send us into the herd of pigs."

He said to them, "Go!" So they came out and went into the pigs, and the whole herd rushed down the steep bank into the lake and died in the water.

—Matthew 8:28-32

Please note that the demon was talking to Jesus and was not fleeing! They were actually having a conversation! The demon only left when Jesus said, "Go!" You are in charge, you have the keys, but you have to speak up! Say something. Again, the Kingdom is a kingdom of laws with proper flow of authority. Your words matter!

Before we move on, let's review what we have learned. When Jesus blessed the bread and fish, they changed kingdoms. And like Jesus, you want to give your seed a directive when you release it. What are you expecting to see once you release your seed? Every seed has a picture attached to it. Every promise carries a picture with it as well. We will talk about this later on, but the next question I want to address is where you should sow your seed.

> **YOU ARE IN CHARGE, YOU HAVE THE KEYS, BUT YOU HAVE TO SPEAK UP!**

Where Should You Sow Your Seed?

First of all, you will want to sow into a God assignment in the earth realm. Please note this is not your normal lifestyle of generosity to those in need type of giving I am talking about.

One who is gracious to a poor man lends to the Lord, and He will repay him for his good deed.

—Proverbs 19:17 (NASB)

It is true that when you are being generous, God will repay you!

Remember this: Whoever sows sparingly will also reap sparingly, and whoever sows generously will also reap generously. Each of you should give what you have decided in your heart to give, not reluctantly or under compulsion, for God loves a cheerful giver. And God is able to bless you abundantly, so that in all things at all times, having all that you need, you will abound in every good work. As it is written:

> *They have freely scattered their gifts to the poor; their righteousness endures forever.*

Now he who supplies seed to the sower and bread for food <u>will also supply and increase your store of seed and will enlarge the harvest of your righteousness. You will be enriched in every way so that you can be generous on every occasion</u>, and through us your generosity will result in thanksgiving to God.

This service that you perform is not only supplying the needs of the Lord's people but is also overflowing in many <u>expressions of thanks to God</u>. Because of the service by which you have proved yourselves, <u>others will praise God</u> for the obedience that accompanies your confession of the gospel of Christ, and <u>for your generosity in sharing with them</u> and with everyone else. And in their prayers for you their hearts will go out to you, because of the *surpassing grace God has given you. Thanks be to God for his indescribable gift!*

—2 Corinthians 9:6-15

Obviously, God rewards those who are generous. But the kind of giving I am talking about is a **targeted giving** with a **targeted harvest**. Remember, I am naming my seed in the type of giving I am talking about. Being generous is an action of compassion, and I usually do not name my generosity giving, but rather, I claim what we have just read in 2 Corinthians 9, that God will give me the seed to be generous and that as I continue to be generous, He will increase my wealth so that I can increase my giving.

Targeted Giving

I have mentioned that when I sow, I am engaged in what I call targeted giving. Again, this giving has a targeted harvest. This is exactly what Jesus did there in Mark chapter 6. He was faced with a very specific need and needed a very specific answer. He needed food to feed those 20,000 people, and so He needed a very specific seed to work with. Now in His case, He was not sowing the seed; He was receiving the seed. And this was not a freewill, give what you want offering. He needed to find someone who would sow a specific seed so it would multiply in God's hands. This is why He said, "Go and see how many loaves you have." Bread and fish were what He needed at the time, not firewood or a cloak but, specifically, bread and fish.

Be sure when you sow, you are giving that directive to meet the specific need you have. When I need something specific, I usually operate in this kind of giving, being clear in what I need, naming my seed as I sow it. When I give, I am usually giving by check or online, so I actually write it on the check. Or if I am giving on the Internet, I will make a notation of what I gave to keep with my records, the directive given to that giving, and the date and time I gave. Remember, you are not looking forward to receiving what you prayed for or declared at a future date; you actually receive those things when you pray!

> *Therefore I tell you, whatever you ask for in prayer, believe that you have received it, and it will be yours.*
>
> —Mark 11:24

Now, this targeted giving is sown into a Kingdom assignment, something that God is doing in the earth realm. It usually is a ministry where God has given a man or woman an assignment that needs funding. Again, this is different than the ordinary helping the poor or needy, which is also God's agenda, of course, and God is very clear on the reward for that type of giving. We are talking about targeted giving. Of course, you can sow this type of giving into your local church, and, in fact, much of your targeted giving should be given to your local church.

Speaking of your home church, your tithe belongs in your local church as well. I have many people ask me if they can tithe to our ministry when they are part of our online church. I tell them, "Of course you can." But I also encourage them to find a great home church in their own area. But if we are their main church home, then yes, they can tithe to us. However, as a pastor, I know people will grow faster and stronger when they are part of a good local church. On the other hand, being part of a church that teaches doubt and unbelief is not a church you want to support or attend.

So as far as sowing into an assignment, you want to sow into agreement, into someone or a ministry that understands faith and that knows what agreement means. Watch out for the, "We are going under if you do not sow" crowd. There is no faith in that statement. The Bible is very clear not to sow while being moved by compulsion. If any man or woman of God makes you feel guilty if you do not sow or they are putting pressure on you to do so, you would be better to just hold on to your money. Faith does not need any prodding.

If you want to sow but really have no leading to give into any particular place, then sow into an assignment that you feel has demonstrated results and teaches faith in what God says. Never sow into a church that says that God kills people or gives them cancer to teach them something or any of that kind of nonsense. But sow into a ministry that teaches the Word of God.

Now, remember to confess or speak over your sowing as you give. Drenda and I have done this since the Lord instructed me how to get my deer that first year. Of course, there was the year I told you about in this chapter where I did not confess over my seed, and you know how that turned out. We consistently spoke over our seed for years without really thinking about it or even knowing it was a vital part of sowing. I assumed that just giving by itself was all that was required to bring my giving under the Kingdom's jurisdiction, and in reality, it does that. But without a clear directive, then there is no focus, no exact harvest; and if you do not know the exact harvest, then you will miss the season of harvest as well.

I have learned many lessons through deer hunting, and as we wind up this chapter on how to release your faith, I wanted to add one more story.

It was just a few years after I had learned how to hunt by faith when for some reason I decided that I would not sow a seed that year. I did not talk about it with my wife; I just did not bring up sowing or praying about the deer as gun season was approaching. I had harvested deer with amazing stories the previous couple of years with what God had taught me, but I guess it was all new to me; and I just felt that I had faith for my own deer then and did not need to go through the motions of releasing my faith. Anyway, you can guess what happened.

Opening morning, I think I saw a buck running that was about 300 yards from me, and that was it. The evening hunt was a bust as well. As I came in the house empty-handed that opening day, Drenda had a friend over at the house as I told her that things were not going well deer hunting. I told her that I had not followed the instructions that God gave me regarding getting my deer. Drenda said, "I was wondering about that when you went out." Well, I acknowledged my error and asked them if they would pray with me about it. I wrote out a check as my seed for the deer, not noting any particular sex. We all laid our hands on it, prayed, and received that deer by faith.

The next day, I could not go out in the morning, so I was going out that evening. I had been eyeing a big maple tree on the property line that I thought would make a good stand, and that is where I headed. It was a very warm evening for December, and if I remember right, it was almost 70 degrees, and it was windy. Just a few minutes into the evening hunt, a huge doe came out of the woods and walked out into the field that the big maple overlooked. The doe was standing broadside to me, giving me a perfect shot. As I sized things up, I realized the doe was about 75 yards from me, and I was a little unsure of the range since I was using a smooth bore 12-gauge. But I took careful aim, and the doe fell at the shot. Boy, was I excited about that one. I got up to the house before dark, and Drenda's friend had come back over; and we all rejoiced in the laws of the Kingdom while at the same time I felt I had learned a lesson.

In this chapter, we have reviewed the second principle of receiving from the Kingdom:

Step #2: Releasing Your Seed into the Kingdom of God

We learned that when we sow our seed into a Kingdom assignment, it changes kingdoms. We also reviewed how we release our seed, <u>with words and with a directive</u>. Here are a few other points we want to remember going forward.

1. We can name money.
2. We can sow for a specific need.
3. We cannot name the tithe.
4. Giving is not a formula; it must be done in faith.
5. Specific giving has a specific harvest.

We release our seed with words.

CHAPTER 6
FAITH IS THE KEY

A few years after we had started our church, I was driving home and was almost to our driveway at the old farmhouse when I saw flashing police lights up ahead. Nothing new, I assumed someone had been pulled over for speeding. Sure enough, as I slowed down, I saw a car in front of the police car slowly pull out and head down the road. As I came up on the police car and slowed down to pass it, something caught my attention. There on the side of the road was a beautiful eight-point buck. I knew in an instant what had happened. The buck had been hit by the car that I saw pull away.

I pulled over just past the buck and walked back to the police car and asked the officer what he was going to do with the buck. Since my driveway was only about 400 yards down the road and I had kids to feed, I thought I would ask if I could have the deer. The police officer seemed relieved to have someone who wanted it. He took my name and my address down and gave me a tag for the deer.

Just before we said good-bye, he told me that they have deer hit all the time, and if I was interested, he would put my name on a list to call if they had a roadkill that no one claimed. I thought that sounded great. It was early fall, and I had not been out hunting yet. This was before I started bowhunting, and gun season was not until the first week of December, so I thought having some venison would be great. Well, it did not take long before I got a call from the police department about another deer. So before gun season ever started, I had already butchered four or five deer. I cannot remember the exact number, but I know it was at least four. The bottom line was my freezers were already full when gun season opened up.

Strangely, Drenda was going to be out of town for the weeklong gun season. I do not remember why she was gone, but I know it was unusual for us to be apart and for a whole week at that. So I did not pray with her about the deer hunting, and I did not even sow a seed. I suppose I was thinking that I did not care if I got a deer since my freezer was full. But I went out; you can be sure of that. To make a long story short, I went out all week during gun season and did not even have a shot. When Drenda got home, she reminded me of what God had already taught me in regard to sowing our seed and praying together to receive our deer.

Well, the next year came around, and this time, I was not going to make the same mistake. Although we did have the police department call us a couple of times regarding roadkill deer, I think I only took one of them as I was planning to get most of my venison from my own hunting. This time, Drenda and I sowed our seed and prayed as we released our seed for a buck. We did not specify what size of buck, just a buck. I was unable to go out opening morning but was excited to go out that evening. But sadly, I must report to you that, again, no deer. I was confused for sure as I made my way to the house that evening after sitting in the woods.

As I sat down to dinner, suddenly, the phone rang. It was the police department stating they had a roadkill if I wanted it. I asked them where it was at, and they gave me the address. I could not believe my ears. "Could you repeat that address again?" I asked. She repeated the address, and I realized it was my own address! I was shocked. So I went to the window, and sure enough, there were red flashing lights at the end of my driveway, so I told them I would be right there. Our driveway was over 900 feet from the road, and I remember I walked that distance in almost complete disbelief. When I got to the deer, it was a very large button buck that was in perfect condition. I filled out some forms, thanked the officer, and then drug the deer up the driveway to the barn. Confused? Very! I did not think anymore about my deer hunting until September or October of the following year.

What Is Your Source?

I cannot remember now which month it was, but I was out jogging around my backfield as I did once in a while to get exercise. As I was jogging, I was praying about what happened the last two years. I just had no clue. Suddenly, as I was running, the words, "the police list" came to me very clearly. I thought for a moment. Was God trying to tell me something? Then I saw it. I realized that my confidence was not in God's Word or His Kingdom. My confidence was in the police list! I knew that if I did not get my own deer, the police department's list would provide one.

Then I also understood why the previous year I received my buck at the end of my driveway instead of at the end of my gun. The police list was where my faith really was. When Drenda and I had sown for that year's buck, the buck showed up right on time the first time out for the year but in the wrong place, or was it? I stood there in awe as the Holy Spirit made it so plain to me. I then understood that the buck showed up exactly where my faith was, the police list. Once I realized that, I ran straight back to the house, immediately called the police department, and took my name off that list. I learned that your backup plan is your real plan! Since that year, I have never failed to see the deer show up every single time.

But how deceptive our hearts are. Our confidence is so easily moved to the natural things. This is something that we need to be aware of and constantly watch out for. Faith does not need a backup plan. I still am amazed that even though my faith was really in the police list, that deer showed up at the end of my driveway that opening day. And this brings up the third principle that God showed me.

Step #3: Release Your Seed When You Are in Faith!

This is a big issue, as we saw earlier when the disciples could not cast the demon out of the demon-possessed boy. Jesus said it was because of their unbelief or lack of faith. Understanding what faith is and how to get faith was covered earlier, but it is vital that you learn to judge yourself, if you are or are not in faith. So let me give you an easy test you can give yourself to see if you are really in faith or not. Close your eyes, and what do you see?

> Now faith is the substance of things hoped for, the evidence of things not seen.
>
> —Hebrews 11:1 (KJV)

Faith is the substance of things hoped for. Hope always carries a picture with it. If I promised you an ice cream cone, you would instantly have a picture of an ice cream cone in your mind. If you believed that I was honest in my offer and I had the means to pay for it, you would see yourself with that ice cream cone, with the evidence of being expedient and excited.

The same is true of the Word of God. When you believe a promise of God and are fully persuaded that God has the intent and the means to make good on His promise, you will see a picture of yourself with the promise. Even though you may not have the promised item at that very moment, you will act like you do, because in a sense you do. The promise is valid, the intent is valid, and it is yours. So faith, being fully persuaded of God's intent and power, is the substance of the promise to you. It is also the evidence of things yet unseen.

> **WHEN YOU BELIEVE A PROMISE OF GOD AND ARE FULLY PERSUADED THAT GOD HAS THE INTENT AND THE MEANS TO MAKE GOOD ON HIS PROMISE, YOU WILL SEE A PICTURE OF YOURSELF WITH THE PROMISE.**

You still need to cash the check, which is a legal process that applies to the spiritual realm as it does in the natural world. So when I say, "Close your eyes. What do you see?" what I am saying is this. If you can't see it, you can't seize it. Let me bring this down to a very simple statement. If you close your eyes and you do not see yourself with the promise, you are not in faith. If you are sick and when you close your eyes, you see yourself healed—I mean you see yourself healed as in no fear, but instead an absolute assurance that you are healed—that is faith. But if you close your eyes and still see yourself sick, waiting to be healed, then you are not in faith. If you need money and you believe a promise of God, then you are no longer anxious about money but you see yourself with the provision you need.

Fear Is the Opposite of Faith

Fear does not exist with this kind of confidence. If you are still nervous about the outcome, you are not in faith. In regard to faith, you need to know how to tell if you are in faith or not. You do not want to make major decisions if you are not in faith, because if you are not in faith, you are in fear. Fear always plays it safe and is unbelief. This is why I said to always sow your seed when you are in faith. You do not want to sow it as a formula, simply going through the motion of giving, because that will not produce anything. You want to be confident of what God says so that when you close your eyes, all you see is you and that promise. You already have it, you possess it, it is yours, and peace has replaced any anxiousness you may have had.

> *Do not be anxious about anything, but in every situation, by prayer and petition, with thanksgiving, present your requests to God. And the peace of God, which transcends all understanding, will guard your hearts and your minds in Christ Jesus.*
> —Philippians 4:6-7

When you are in faith, there is a peace that is not based on circumstances but on the promise.

Next, an evidence of faith is your ability to defend yourself in a spiritual court of law. Since faith is based on the Word of God, you must know why you believe what you believe. Pretend you are in a courtroom and you are the defense attorney. The prosecution is stating that your client is living in their client's home illegally and is stating that the house actually does not belong to your client but is owned by their client. What would you do? Say you are sorry and that your client will vacate the property immediately? If you have the signed deed in your possession, fear would be replaced by confidence, and you would tell the judge to throw those imposters out of the courtroom. This is how faith acts. It knows the truth, is confident, and comes across almost as arrogant. So can you defend your position?

Sarah came to our church one day not knowing where she was as she was in a new town just driving around. She and her husband had been transferred to Columbus, and they had been praying about finding a church. As they were driving around, they turned around in our driveway and thought they may as well try us out. They never left. Sarah suffered from asthma her entire life. In and out of the hospitals growing up, her life was held hostage by the disease. She learned how to avoid certain environments that caused her asthma to flare up, and she carried her inhaler everywhere she went.

At Faith Life Church, she learned that healing was her legal right and how to defend herself spiritually. One service as she was listening to one of our members describe how they had been healed of a life-threatening disease, she made up her mind. God is no respecter of persons. She removed her inhaler from her purse and replaced it with Scripture cards, all describing her legal right to be healed. She would read them every day. Whenever she felt an asthma attack coming on, she would reach for a Scripture card instead of her inhaler, and she has never had an asthma attack again!

My aunt came to me at a family reunion. She asked me if I would pray for her as she had lung cancer and was facing surgery in a week and a half to remove a large tumor. She went on to tell me that her doctors had been tracking a grapefruit size tumor that was in her lungs for a year and a half. It had suddenly begun to grow more quickly, and the doctors said it had to come out. As I stood there listening to her story, I reflected on her life. She was a chain smoker all her life, and I knew that she had not been to church for many years. I promised her that I would indeed pray for her but felt she was not ready for prayer at that moment. I asked her if she would read some material that I wanted to give her concerning healing before I prayed. I said I would be glad to pray for her that coming Sunday morning right after the worship service. She agreed.

I knew that she had given her heart to the Lord years ago but had not lived for Him. I hoped that taking the time to reflect on God's promises of healing would encourage her faith. I also knew we had a much better chance of seeing a positive result if we could pray in agreement with the Word of God as the anchor and the hope in which we were placing our trust.

So the following Sunday, my aunt came to church just like she said she would. After the worship service, I asked her to come forward; and as she stood there, I asked her if she had read the material I gave her. She said she had, so I then asked her, "How do you know you will be healed when I lay my hands on you?" She then quoted several Scriptures and stated that her confidence was in the Word of God. I knew at that moment she was ready for prayer, and I laid my hands on her, prayed, and declared she was healed and free of cancer. The anointing of God came on her as I prayed, and she collapsed to the floor under the power of God. As she got up, she was trembling as she exclaimed, "I am healed!"

She went into surgery on that Tuesday to have the tumor removed, but when they went in, there was nothing there. No tumor, not even a scar or indication that there was ever anything there.

It is so strange to watch people live their lives. You would think that my aunt would have been so grateful that God healed her that she never would have missed a day of church for the rest of her life.

But that was not the case. I think I saw her only one time after that Sunday. She died about six or seven years later from a different type of cancer. But this time, she never asked me to pray for her.

Hold on to the Moment When You Released Your Faith

One thing that I remind people is that there is always time between the "Amen" and the "There it is." Because of this, it is vital that you hold on to the moment of faith's release. I suggest that you write this down in your journal or on a note to remind yourself. I mentioned this earlier, but I believe it is so important. An example of what I might write down is as follows. "On November 12th at 1:30 p.m., I believe that I received a (insert the specific request) according to Mark 11:24, and I believe that I received when I prayed." You can add other notes like who agreed with you, the amount you sowed, and to what God assignment you sowed it. That is just an example, but it is important to write it down because you can fight with that.

> THERE IS ALWAYS TIME BETWEEN THE "AMEN" AND THE "THERE IT IS." BECAUSE OF THIS, IT IS VITAL THAT YOU HOLD TO ON THE MOMENT OF FAITH'S RELEASE.

When circumstances tempt you to retreat in fear, you can remind yourself of the date and time you received your answer. When fear would try to rise up, I would take that note out and read it out loud as a declaration. "No, Fear, you are a liar. I already have received that on this date and time according to (and then insert the Scripture you are standing on.)" Sometimes I would have to read that note several times to keep my heart quiet and in peace. Do not allow what may appear as a failure to lure you into letting go of your faith. In fact, this principle was so important while my kids were growing up that in our weekly family prayer meeting we would have a family journal where we would write what we had prayed about and what we were believing we had received. We called this our James 4 notebook. In fact, we sell them through the ministry if you would like one.

Sometimes, there are things happening in the Spirit that you are not aware of. God is working to orchestrate everything, but it may take time. There may be many pieces to the puzzle that must be put in place. For instance, if God is going to meet a financial need, He may have to speak to someone to take care of that or bring you an opportunity to capture the money you need. Again, that all takes time.

> *Do not be afraid, Daniel. Since the first day that you set your mind to gain understanding and to humble yourself before your God, your words were heard, and I have come in response to them. But the prince of the Persian kingdom resisted me twenty-one days. Then Michael, one of the chief princes, came to help me, because I was detained there with the king of Persia. Now I have come to explain to you what will happen to your people in the future, for the vision concerns a time yet to come.*
> —Daniel 10:12-14

Let's take another look at the campus story I told you about earlier. We had looked at various buildings and considered leasing space in several of them but did not feel to move on one of them. When we first launched out to find a campus, we sowed a seed for God to show us the perfect place. Every time we found a location and considered it, we felt a check in our spirits, and we almost grew discouraged. We checked every building in the area where we wanted to put our campus, but there were not any available options that we felt good about.

Our core values as a church include a strong desire to help educate children and take care of families. We have talked many times about possibly someday having a school, having a day care center, a latchkey program, and many more programs to minister to our communities. Our current space is maxed out, which prohibited our pursuit of any of those options.

You could say it may have looked like the Kingdom was not coming through, but you must remember that we had already sown for the perfect campus. The reality was that God knew the school we purchased was going into foreclosure. He saw the big picture. That property was not available when we first started looking.

Besides knowing that the school would be our perfect campus, He also knew how we were going to pay for it. The couple that actually bought the campus for us was on my calendar at least four times for a dinner. Due to various circumstances, we both had to move that dinner engagement until the night that we met. We had just seen the property the morning of the exact day we had dinner with them.

There were others who wanted the school, but we were the first to put in a bid. Everything was timed perfectly. When we sowed that $100,000 two days before we had that dinner, by the instruction of the Holy Spirit, I believe that Satan was going to try to keep that school hidden from us or use some other tactic to keep it from us. When God told me to sow that money and to rebuke Satan from interfering with us finding our campus, I believe that some plan that he had to interfere was stopped.

The couple who provided the cash to purchase the property was also in the middle of making a decision on whether to help a friend with the purchase of a property, which would have used the available cash that they used for our purchase. After they heard our story that night, they said that they then understood why they did not have peace to fund the friend's purchase. So just remember, when you pray in faith, knowing that you receive when you pray, there is still time between the "Amen" and "There it is." So stay strong and be patient.

Stand Firm on Your Faith

But let patience have her perfect work, that ye may be perfect and entire, wanting nothing.

—James 1:4 (KJV)

This is why I suggest to people that they note the date and time they release their faith, because you need to stand.

When my daughter was facing a 13-pound tumor in her abdomen, she grew tired of putting up with the health issues it was causing: constant infections in her kidneys, constant backaches, and digestive issues. She decided that enough was enough, and she decided to take 30 days to just meditate on the Word of God and God's promises concerning healing. At the end of that season, she asked her mother and me to lay hands on her as she believed she was healed. So the elders of our church and her mother and I laid our hands on her and believed that she was healed according to James 5:14-16.

Is anyone among you sick? Let them call the elders of the church to pray over them and anoint them with oil in the name of the Lord. And the prayer offered in faith will make the sick person well; the Lord will raise them up. If they have sinned, they will be forgiven. Therefore confess your sins to each other and pray for each other so that you may be healed. The prayer of a righteous person is powerful and effective.

—James 5:14-16

She went home that night the same way she had come in; the tumor was still there. But she said, "I am healed." She held to her confession for two weeks with no change, even though she was in the worst pain she had ever been in. She told me that during that two-week period while she was in such pain, she told Satan, "You can try and hurt me, but I am healed."

Two weeks later, she went to bed with that tumor still there, but she woke up completely healed. She lost 13 pounds and 9 inches in her waist as she slept, and her back, which was knotted and twisted, was recreated into a perfect spine.

Once you are confident of the promise, do not let Satan deceive you out of your healing or out of any promise that God has given you.

Christine came to our church without much of a church background. It was all new to her. Christine had worn two hearing aids for years and lost a large majority of her hearing during that time. Her mother had the same disease and was almost totally deaf.

When Christine attended our church, she gave her heart to the Lord, and God dramatically changed her life. She was excited and wanted to learn as much as she could about the Kingdom of God. We have a believers' orientation class for those that are new to the church, and Christine was eager to attend. The classes cover various topics, but it just so happened that the class that Christine was attending was on healing. At the end of the session, the leaders offered prayer for those that needed healing. Christine was so excited as she went forward for prayer. As she was being prayed for, her ears suddenly popped open. For the first time, she could hear perfectly.

As she was leaving service that day, I felt led to warn her of what I call Satan's counterattack. Sure enough, she said the next morning,

AGAIN, STANDING STRONG ON THE WORD OF GOD IS A KEY TO YOUR FREEDOM.

suddenly, her ears popped shut, and she was tempted to become concerned. But I told her this was going to happen, and when it did, she was to declare that she was healed and to rebuke Satan. Well, she did exactly what I told her to do. She began to praise God and declared that she was healed as she bound the enemy. In a few minutes, her ears popped open and have been open ever since, and that was about four years ago.

Again, standing strong on the Word of God is a key to your freedom.

I'll Say It Again—Be Specific

In regard to releasing your faith, let me remind you one more time to be specific! This story is when God really showed me the importance of my words. I have told it for years, but it is as powerful today as it was when it happened.

It was a normal deer season, and I was so ready to get out in the woods as things had been so busy. This particular year, I had sowed seed for two bucks, one a buck with four-point or bigger antlers and the second a button buck. Drenda and I sowed our seed in agreement and in faith. I went out on the first hunt in the morning while it was still barely light. As the sky was just getting pink, I had my buck, an eight-point buck. The total time in my tree was 15 minutes! Pretty exciting! So when I went out two weeks later to get my button buck, I was very confident. Again, I went out in the morning, and about 20 minutes into the morning, I spotted an eight-point buck about 300 yards away heading straight for my tree.

In Ohio, you can only harvest one buck with antlers. The second deer has to be a doe or a button buck. Button bucks count as does because the antlers are so small you really cannot see them from a distance. So when I saw the buck coming across the field, I assumed he would turn off before he got to my tree, but he didn't. He came straight to my tree and stood still under my stand for about 20 seconds. All I could do was watch as he was not legal. After standing there for those 20 seconds, he suddenly just started to walk back down the same trail he had come on. Amazingly, he walked the same 300 yards back across that field and disappeared. I was shocked and confused.

Now, I had never had a deer come under my stand that was not the exact deer that I had sown my seed for. I was confused and began to pray in the Spirit as I walked back to the house. "Lord, why was that buck there?" Suddenly, I heard the Holy Spirit say, "Check your seed." Check my seed? That is crazy; I know what I sowed for. Nevertheless, the bank that I use sends copies of the canceled checks with the monthly statements. I quickly grabbed the statement and found my check. On the bottom of the check, I had written, two bucks four-point or bigger, one button buck. How many deer is that? What I meant to say was I was believing for two bucks total, one with four points or bigger and the other a button buck. The way I wrote it, however, indicated that I was sowing for two bucks that had four points or more and one button buck. I sat there stunned. That second buck came because I had sown a seed for him. That is why he came across that field and stood under my tree. He was supposed to be there.

When I saw that, I started yelling and shouting and running around the house. I was so excited, but at the same time, it scared me. How many times had I said things that I did not really want to come to pass but had put them into motion with my words? This certainly made James 3:3-4 come to life.

> *When we put bits into the mouths of horses to make them obey us, we can turn the whole animal. Or take ships as an example. Although they are so large and are driven by strong winds, they are steered by a very small rudder wherever the pilot wants to go.*
> —James 3:3-4

James is speaking of how powerful our words are. It is clear if our words are saying one thing while we really want to see something else, we will find our lives shipwrecked and not know how we got there.

So remember, the Kingdom is very specific, and your words define exactly where you go and how you get there!

The Importance of Agreement

We are still talking about releasing your seed when you are in faith, and here is something you need to remember. If you are married, be in agreement with your spouse. If you do not have a spouse, I will address that in a minute, but let's assume you are married. Again, stay in agreement with your spouse.

Early in my marriage, I hated to ask Drenda to agree with me concerning my hunting. The reason was because if I talked about going hunting, I knew she would say something about the trash that needed taken out, the light bulb that should be changed, or a list of other things that needed done. Now, this was when I was immature and selfish. She had been with the children all day, but the minute I got home, I wanted to go out into the woods. I do not think God will bless that attitude. Yes, I was selfish. Before I learned how to hunt by faith, I would spend days hunting with no success. It was no wonder she dreaded hunting season.

But I learned to put her first. I had to learn that we were in this thing together and we needed each other. As I began to put her needs first, she was more than willing to agree with me for the deer. But she was especially happy to see me have success with my deer hunting. I had to learn that as husband and wife, we were one spiritually and there was nothing more powerful than when we both came together in agreement. It was not just about the deer hunting. I found out that if we walked together in unity, it worked in every area of life.

> **I HAD TO LEARN THAT AS HUSBAND AND WIFE, WE WERE ONE SPIRITUALLY AND THERE WAS NOTHING MORE POWERFUL THAN WHEN WE BOTH CAME TOGETHER IN AGREEMENT.**

> *Husbands, in the same way be considerate as you live with your wives, and treat them with respect as the weaker partner and as heirs with you of the gracious gift of life, so that nothing will hinder your prayers.*

—1 Peter 3:7

Notice, men, that if you are not considerate with your wives, your prayers will be hindered! Considerate means that you view her as an equal, as you are one with her in every decision. Yes, spiritually, the man is the head of the marriage but not in the form of a dictator but as a servant, laying down his life for her and honoring her.

What If Your Spouse Isn't a Believer?

I get emails asking what people should do if they are married to a spouse that does not want to serve the Lord. How can they be in agreement? Your understanding of agreement is faulty. Let's say that you are married to a man who does not serve the Lord. You both, however, agree that you need a new car. Guess what? You are in agreement! If you both agree that you need groceries, then you are in agreement. The Bible is very clear that if just one of the union believes the Word of God, then the Kingdom has legal jurisdiction to work in the family!

> For the unbelieving husband has been sanctified through his wife, and the unbelieving wife has been sanctified through her believing husband. Otherwise your children would be unclean, but as it is, they are holy.
> —1 Corinthians 7:14

I do not believe that this is saying that the unbelieving spouse is saved by their spouse's faith. I believe that each person must call on the name of Jesus personally. However, I do believe that if one spouse believes the Word of God, their faith sanctifies or brings the entire family under the blessing of the Kingdom. Now, obviously, being married to a believing spouse is better, of course. And the Bible is clear in encouraging the believing spouse with the truth that their faith can win their unbelieving spouse to the Kingdom.

If you are not married, you do not need to find another person to agree with you in prayer. You just believe the Word for yourself and watch the Kingdom work!

While we are on the topic of faith, I would like to discuss in the next chapter probably one of the most common questions I get asked about sowing and the mistake so many people make.

CHAPTER 7
WARNING: STAY WITHIN YOUR DEVELOPED FAITH!

"I am going to catch a 900-pound marlin!" That was the comment from one of my associates who was going on the trip to Maui, Hawaii, with my office. It was an all-expenses paid trip that we had won by our production with one of our vendors. Before heading out for Maui, three of us decided to go fishing for blue marlin, as it is no secret that Maui is known as the blue marlin capital of the world. We had been talking about faith months before this event, and I was teaching the guys how it worked. Dan was new to the world of faith, and I remember thinking that this was a great opportunity for him to step out and see the Kingdom work firsthand. So I said to him, "Hey, Dan, did you know it is possible to know without any doubt that you will catch a blue marlin when we go to Hawaii?" That comment got his attention, and we spent many hours discussing faith before we left for Maui. Dan sowed his seed just like I had taught him and was so excited to go after his dream, a blue marlin.

My other associate was a member of my church, already had a good understanding of how faith worked, and had seen God do amazing things in his life. He also sowed his seed toward catching a marlin, not just any marlin but a 900-pound marlin. I remember thinking, "Wow, that is a big fish!" I had some concern about the very specific size of fish that my friend was sowing for, but I did not say anything about it to him at the time.

Dan, on the other hand, did not sow toward any particular size of fish. Well, to make a long story short, Dan caught a 167-pound blue marlin, but my other associate did not catch a marlin at all. So why did Dan catch his marlin but my other friend did not? This is a good question, and most people, even most Christians, would be shocked at even asking it. They would laugh and say, "Fishing is a sometimes you catch them and sometimes you don't proposition." But I learned that the Kingdom is very specific and reliable.

> *One day as Jesus was standing by the Lake of Gennesaret, the people were crowding around him and listening to the word of God. He saw at the water's edge two boats, left there by the fishermen, who were washing their nets. He got into one of the boats, the one belonging to Simon, and asked him to put out a little from shore. Then he sat down and taught the people from the boat.*
>
> *When he had finished speaking, he said to Simon, "Put out into deep water, and let down the nets for a catch."*
>
> *Simon answered, "Master, we've worked hard all night and haven't caught anything. But because you say so, I will let down the nets."*
>
> *When they had done so, they caught such a large number of fish that their nets began to break. So they signaled their partners in the other boat to come and help them, and they came and filled*

both boats so full that they began to sink.

When Simon Peter saw this, he fell at Jesus' knees and said, "Go away from me, Lord; I am a sinful man!" For he and all his companions were astonished at the catch of fish they had taken, and so were James and John, the sons of Zebedee, Simon's partners.

—Luke 5:1-10

Peter discovered a new way of fishing, just as I had deer hunting. He had tried fishing but caught no fish until Jesus told him where to fish, in the deep water. There he caught so many fish that his two boats almost sank. I tell people, "Anyone can catch fish if Jesus tells you where and how to fish."

So in regard to my friend that did not catch his big marlin, yes, it is true that all things are possible to you with God. But if you sowed a seed believing to catch a blue marlin in your bathtub, you would know that would not work. Now, if you wanted to catch a blue marlin, you could sow a seed, and the Holy Spirit would lead to where you could catch one—in the ocean, of course, but where in the ocean?

Remember this: Every harvest has a unique location and timing for the harvest! If you wanted to sow for a world record blue marlin, you could not just say, "I will go to the ocean." You would have to go to a specific area in the ocean. Why? Because blue marlin migrate and have certain routes they take every year. Catching a 900-pound blue marlin is also rare. For instance, the Emerald Coast Blue Marlin Classic fishing tournament in Miramar, Florida, has been running for 17 years. The largest blue marlin ever caught during that time was 899 pounds. Was it possible to catch a 900-pound blue marlin on that trip to Maui? Possibly, since the record blue marlin caught in Hawaii was 1,376 pounds, but write this down.

The more specific or unique the object of your faith is, the more important it is to pay attention to the location, method, and timing.

The captain of the boat that day in Maui told us that the blue marlin were not there yet. He owned two boats that had been out eight hours a day for the prior four months but had only caught one striped marlin. The blue marlin were due later in the month. Of course, we caught the first one of the season. But when my friend made his seed more specific, and especially set at a record book level marlin, the more critical the location and timing would be to the harvest. I personally believe there just was not a record size marlin in the area at the time. We also need to realize it's possible that my friend was not really in faith for the big fish. But if he is really serious about catching a 900-pound marlin, then I know if he sows his seed and listens to the Holy Spirit as far as location is concerned, and listens for the correct timing, he will get his 900-pound blue marlin.

Location and Timing Matter

Being specific in the location and timing of the harvest is just as important as the very specific seed you sow. You saw this play out when I did the seven-point buck experiment. I had to wait until I had the unction to go out; and in that case, I waited for over a month during the hunting season. Why? Most likely because the seven-point was not on my property yet or maybe other factors that could have been a deterrent to my success were present, such as weather and wind direction.

The Holy Spirit knew the timing for that specific harvest, and he put me in the right stand, on the right day, at the right time to harvest that exact deer.

I hear and see this error often. "Hey, Gary, if the Kingdom brings the deer in like you say, why don't you just go out and kill the world record buck?" Okay, good question, and we need to address it. That statement is like emails I get from people wanting to pay off a $500,000 mortgage and they tell me they sowed a seed for it to be paid off in seven days. When it does not show up in seven days, they get discouraged and ask me why the money didn't show up. Another common question I hear is, "Why can't I just sow a seed and win the lottery?"

> LET ME SAY IT AGAIN—I THINK YOU NEED TO HEAR IT AGAIN—GOD HAS YOUR PLAN!

Okay, let's talk about the record buck question first. Yes, I believe that I could kill the record buck if that was a passion for me, which it is not. I usually hunt for meat, and I am not motivated to go after a record buck. One of the reasons I am not motivated to go after that world record buck is because of what I have just explained to you; you will not catch a whale in your bathtub. The world record buck is not on my property. If I was really serious about harvesting that buck, then I know I would have to go somewhere else to hunt. I might possibly need to learn some new tactics as record bucks are usually nocturnal and have their own unique habits. I would have to do a lot of research and praying to locate the area where such an animal would be found. But I do not want to go to all that trouble. I like hunting in my own woods. I love going out in my own backyard and getting a good eating deer in the comfort of my own woods. But to answer your question, I believe a person could believe God for that buck, but remember what I said. The more unique and specific the harvest, the more important are the location, timing, and method.

Usually, when I get an email from someone asking me why a million dollars did not show up in five days, I realize that I am probably, not always, talking to a person who has not learned the difference between being in faith and being presumptuous.

It is like the email I got one day saying they were going to sow a seed for ten million dollars in 30 days when they did not even have groceries, had not paid their rent for three months, and had no job. They were way outside of their developed faith.

So, Gary, are you saying that God could not give someone ten million dollars? Of course He could. All things are possible with God. The question is not "Can He?" but "Do you really have faith for that?" If your faith can't bring in the food you need, I doubt you have faith for that ten million dollars at this point in your life. But you can get there! You have to start where you are and begin to learn how faith works and also expand your capacity to manage more than you are managing now.

Can You Believe to Win the Lottery?

What about the lottery?

Wow, let's go ahead and jump into this one. Those Powerball jackpots have really gotten huge over the last few years. I remember this past year it reached almost one billion dollars! I had never bought a lottery ticket in my life, but this time, when it was at one billion, a couple of us in the office said, "Hey, let's at least buy a couple of tickets." I did not think much of it, so I thought that I might as well throw in a couple of dollars. I knew the odds—I wasn't putting any confidence in winning—but I guess I just figured that I would throw my money in the pot. Like everyone was saying, "Someone has to win it." I guess I thought that when someone won that one billion dollars, I did not want to think that I missed out on at least having a dollar in the running. Well, I am embarrassed to say that I actually fell for it.

That night, the Lord spoke to me in a dream about it. He simply said in my dream, "All my promises are yours!" "Yes, Sir, I hear you loud and clear," I said. "I understand." Yes, He corrected me, but He also encouraged me. He let me know that I do not need that lottery, and if I need a billion dollars, He will provide it when I need it. I have over 7,000 promises that I have a legal claim to, and they are more than enough!

Now, back to answering that question about sowing to win the lottery or any contest; you do not have jurisdiction over it. I can sow for a deer because deer are subject to man. I have legal jurisdiction over them. But I have no jurisdiction over the lottery; it is a game of chance.

How to Tell When You Are Not in Faith

Learning to judge if you are in faith will help you when you make decisions and help you recognize not to make a decision if you are in fear. Remember, faith is confident, expectant, and full of peace. Confidence was something I did not have when I launched out to harvest my first trophy buck. I was not in faith. Can you tell when you are not in faith? I hope so.

As you know, Drenda and I own 60 beautiful acres with a mix of woods, marsh, and grassland. It is an absolutely perfect place to hunt deer. There are crops planted all around our property, and the woods and marsh are natural magnets for the deer. I built my office over our garage with wooden bookshelves and a built-in gas fireplace. It is a quiet, cozy man cave type of office, from which I love to work. The only thing that was missing was a nice mounted buck over my desk. To be truthful about it, I was never interested in shooting big bucks as I was a meat hunter, and I had never shot a buck that really was big enough to warrant mounting. But the more I thought about it, I agreed with Drenda, as she was the one that insisted I shoot a big buck for my office.

We had lived on the property for five years when we had this discussion, and I had never seen a big buck on the property. I had been out every deer season and had shot a couple of nice eight-point bucks but nothing that I would consider mounting class. But that year, I told Drenda that I thought I would go for the big buck for the wall. Again, I had never seen a big buck in the woods. Our kitchen window faces the woods and the field, and yet, I had never seen one.

But Drenda and I sowed for the big buck. I wrote on my seed check that I was sowing for a 10-point or bigger. We prayed over that seed, and I laid it on my desk to mail. That envelope sat there for three days, and I just couldn't mail it. I knew that I did not have

IT IS ALREADY ALL YOURS, MY FRIEND, THE ENTIRE KINGDOM. GOD CANNOT ADD ANYTHING TO WHAT HE HAS ALREADY GIVEN YOU. YOU ALREADY HAVE IT ALL!

faith for that 10-point. I had faith for an eight, six, or four-point all day long. But I was having trouble seeing that big buck with that assurance of faith that says, "I know that I know that I will shoot a 10-point or bigger buck when I go out." I had enough experience with the Kingdom to know that I was not in faith. So I tore that check up, replaced it with a check that said "for a four-point or bigger," and mailed it off.

The night before I was going out, I told Drenda what I had done. "I just do not have faith for that big buck," I told her. She looked at me and said, "You have faith for the deer, and I will have faith for the trophy buck. God is able to do immeasurably more than all you ask or think!"

The morning opened with the usual rustling of squirrels and birds in the woods as the smell of fall leaves took me back in my mind to many deer hunts. I hadn't sat there very long, maybe 20 minutes, when I heard the sound of a buck coming through the woods. The buck was heading straight for my tree like clockwork, and I readied myself for the shot. As the buck got closer, I saw that the buck was a four-point, exactly what I usually go for as they are very good eating. The buck stepped into an opening at about 25 yards, and I let the arrow go. With disgust, I saw the arrow hit high and back, and I knew that I would have to track this one. The buck took off through the woods and then jumped into the cornfield that bordered the woods and was out of sight. I could still hear it running through the corn and knew from how strong it was running that I might have a long tracking job ahead of me.

I waited in the tree stand for about 20 minutes and then decided to get down out of the tree to inspect the arrow. Sure enough, I could tell I definitely hit the buck, and I spotted a trail of blood. As I followed the blood trail, I was encouraged as there was a good trail of blood. But after about 100 yards, the blood trail dried up. I looked and looked but could not find another drop. After two hours of looking, I realized that the buck was gone. I was so disappointed. One, I do not ever want to wound a deer and lose it; and secondly, I was disappointed with my shot.

As I stood there in the cornfield, I started to walk back toward the house when I had a thought. *I still have a chance. I may jump a deer as I make my way home through the cornfield and then the marsh area.* I loaded my crossbow. As I slowly made my way along the weeded gully in the cornfield, suddenly, a deer jumped up and dashed out in front of me. Not knowing what I was, the deer stopped and looked back. Since I had camouflage on, the deer, which I could see was a buck, hesitated as it could not make me out. It all happened in a split second. I could see antlers, although I could not tell how big or how many points there were. I knew that I had but a split second to make up my mind about the buck. He was beyond my normal bow range at about 55 yards and standing broadside to me. I quickly pulled up and aimed at the top of his back and let the arrow go. The buck dropped instantly as the arrow hit and stayed down. I was kind of in shock. Did that really just happen?

As I walked up to the buck, the first thing I said was, "Drenda's faith!" The buck was huge! I counted 26 points, and he had drop tines as well. I had never seen a buck as big as this one. Well, to say I was thrilled would not give the moment justice. As you can guess, the buck is now over my desk in my office. But I want to talk about this deer for a minute. How or why did he show up?

The four-point showed up right on time even though I messed up the shot. But Drenda said she was believing for the trophy buck. Now, she had an advantage over me. She does not hunt deer, and to her, a trophy buck should be as easy as a four-point. They are just deer to her. Because she does not hunt, she did not have an arguing picture of impossibility talking back to her. I had never even seen a big eight-point on the property, but her faith was not based on what was on the property or not. She believed that God could bring it.

This hunt took place during the deer breeding season, the rut as it is called, and bucks can travel for miles looking for does. So there is always a good chance you will see bucks that you normally do not see on your property in the rut, as was the case here.

Partnering in Faith

Drenda's faith brought that buck in even though I had no faith for the trophy buck. I want you to read that again. I had no faith for that trophy buck! I know what you are thinking. "Hold on, Gary. I am confused. If you had no faith for that buck, then why did it show up?" Let me show you.

> One day as Jesus was standing by the Lake of Gennesaret, the people were crowding around him and listening to the word of God. He saw at the water's edge two boats, left there by the fishermen, who were washing their nets. He got into one of the boats, the one belonging to Simon, and asked him to put out a little from shore. Then he sat down and taught the people from the boat.
>
> When he had finished speaking, he said to Simon, "Put out into deep water, and let down the nets for a catch."
>
> Simon answered, "Master, we've worked hard all night and haven't caught anything. But because you say so, I will let down the nets."
>
> When they had done so, they caught such a large number of fish that their nets began to break. So they signaled their partners in the other boat to come and help them, and they came and filled both boats so full that they began to sink.
>
> —Luke 5:1-7

I know we already looked at this story earlier, but I wanted to point out something here that will answer our question.

> *When they had done so, they caught such a large number of fish that their nets began to break.* ***So they signaled their partners in the other boat to come and help them, and they came and filled both boats so full that they began to sink.***

I want to ask you a question. How much faith did James and John use to fill their boat with fish? The answer is none! If you remember, Peter's boat, as well as James and John's boat was on shore, and they were washing their nets when Jesus came by. Jesus asked Peter for the use of his boat to preach from and then afterward told him to cast his net over in the deep water for a catch of fish. The result was that Peter caught so many fish that his nets began to break and his boat began to sink. Peter called to his partners who were on the shore to come and help bring in the fish. Their boat filled exactly as Peter's had, to overflowing. My question to you is, "How much faith did James and John use to fill their boat?" The answer is none. Then why did their boat have exactly the same catch as Peter's? The text answers that question; it says they were partners.

I ALWAYS SAY THAT GOD'S SECRETS ARE HIDDEN FOR YOU, NOT FROM YOU! SATAN DWELLS IN DARKNESS AND DOES NOT KNOW THE PLANS OF GOD.

The definition of partner in the Collins English Dictionary is: "A person who shares or is associated with another in some action or endeavor; usually sharing its risks and profits."

A partnership is a legal entity and shares in the risks, costs, and profit of the business. So when Peter's faith followed Jesus, he was really loaning Jesus the business in a legal sense, not just the boat. Technically, James and John also owned a part of the boat that Peter let Jesus use, and because of that, both boats filled equally. So whose faith was it that brought that harvest? Obviously, it was Peter's. He is the one who said, "Master, we've worked hard all night and haven't caught anything. <u>But because you say so</u>, I will let down the nets."

So James and John reaped exactly the same harvest as Peter did even though they did not exercise faith in that situation. So it was with Drenda. We are partners, and we are one. Her faith, by itself, brought that buck in that day. You can see that this concept of partnership is a powerful spiritual principle, as we have just seen in this story. Paul talked about this principle of partnership in the book of Philippians.

> *I thank my God every time I remember you. In all my prayers for all of you, I always pray with joy because of your partnership in the gospel from the first day until now, being confident of this, that he who began a good work in you will carry it on to completion until the day of Christ Jesus.*
>
> *It is right for me to feel this way about all of you, since I have you in my heart and, whether I am in chains or defending and confirming the gospel, <u>all of you share in God's grace with me</u>.*
> —Philippians 1:3-7

Paul says he remembers the church at Philippi with joy because of their continuing partnership with his ministry. He goes on to state that because of their partnership, they now share in God's grace that is on his ministry. Grace is God's empowerment or God's ability that was on Paul to accomplish his assignment. The church at Philippi was sharing the expense of the assignment, and like James and John, they also shared in the anointing and grace that was on that assignment. Let's go over to chapter 4, and you will see the amazing result that partnership produces.

> *Yet it was good of you to share in my troubles. Moreover, as you Philippians know, in the early days of your acquaintance with the gospel, when I set out from Macedonia, not one church shared with me in the matter of giving and receiving, except you only; for even when I was in Thessalonica, you sent me aid more than once when I was in need. Not that I desire your gifts; what I desire is that more be credited to your account. I have received full payment and have more than enough. I am amply supplied, now that I have received from Epaphroditus the gifts you sent. They are a fragrant offering, an acceptable sacrifice, pleasing to God. And my God will meet all your needs according to the riches of his glory in Christ Jesus.*
>
> —Philippians 4:14-19

Pay close attention to what Paul says to the church in Philippi, "My God will meet all your needs." Notice that Paul did not say, "Your God will meet your needs because you have been generous to me." NO! He said, "My God will now meet your needs!" You see, the Philippians were partners with Paul, and as partners, they shared in the grace on Paul's assignment. Now, like James and John catching all those fish because of Peter's faith, Paul is declaring that their needs will be met because of his faith! I hope you can see the advantage of this principle.

Let's assume you need a car and you partner with us as a ministry.

Let's also assume the car costs $30,000. Now, when you sow into Garykeesee.com, you understand what partnership means. You share in the anointing and grace on our ministry. As a ministry, we can easily agree on that $30,000 because we passed needing $30,000 a long time ago. We can easily have faith for $30,000 as we spend millions annually now. But back in the day, I can remember having to believe God for $30,000, which at the time seemed like a huge mountain. So if you ask me if I could believe God for $30,000, the answer would be "Absolutely." So like Paul, when we are in agreement and we are partners, I can declare that your need is met not because of your faith but because of mine.

Now obviously, you need to be in faith when you sow the seed toward that $30,000, and you have to have confidence not only in the Word of God but also in me. You should have faith in me, be confident that I am anointed and called of God, that I operate in integrity, and you should be able to see demonstrated results in my life and in my ministry. If you looked at what we are doing and where we came from, you know I have faith for $30,000! You may not have $30,000 faith, but we can work together in partnership and see things that are amazing. It was the same for the trophy buck. Drenda said the night before I went out, "You believe for the deer, and I will believe for the trophy buck." This is how partnership works.

Choosing Strategic Partnerships

So let me lay some ground rules here by asking you a question. If you were going to start a computer company, would you want a guy who was in his first semester of computer science classes with no money to be your partner or someone who had built a multimillion dollar computer business and had the finances to help with your company launch? Of course, there are many variables here, and I am only making an illustration. But I think on the surface the obvious choice would be someone that has experience, has a proven track record, and was not going broke!

Well, the same is true when you want to sow into a ministry partnership. Please do not confuse what I am saying in regard to a direct leading of God to partner with someone. That kind of leading supersedes what I am talking about. Many times, God will lead you to partner with His assignments, but sometimes you get to pick. I am talking specifically about sowing as a choice you make, sowing when you are desiring to move to the next level. I know I sow into assignments that I believe in for the express purpose of accelerating the funds needed in my own life. One rule I do not break is I always sow into an assignment that understands faith and agreement unless I am sowing to the poor or needy. Of course, we do not expect the poor and needy to understand faith. We are sowing love to them, and God will repay us. Again, sowing to the poor is a different type of sowing than we have been talking about here. Another thing I will look for when I sow is locating a God assignment that has the same fruit that I am believing God for myself.

For instance, my company owns two airplanes. Before I bought either one of them, I sowed into a God assignment, a ministry that I knew had paid for many multimillion dollar planes in the past. When I say many, I mean many, and they were all paid for with cash. They had a demonstrated result when it came to planes. I knew they could easily agree with me for a plane and be in faith for it to come to pass. I wasn't going to partner with a ministry that said planes were too expensive or not worth owning. That is not any kind of agreement. No, I wanted to be in agreement with a ministry that understood where I was, could relate to me believing God for a plane, and had the fruit to prove it.

I have been a pilot since I was 19 years old and learned to fly off of a 3,000-foot gravel runway out in the country. I rented planes all my life until one day I thought, *Hey, you know what? I just need to sow a seed and believe God for my own plane.* Well, that is just what I did. I knew the exact plane I was going to sow for. So I wrote that exact plane on my check, and Drenda and I agreed on it. We then sent that check to the ministry that I just mentioned.

Well, about a month went by, and I had a routine doctor's visit. As I was talking to the doctor that day, he casually said, "Do you happen to know anyone who would like to buy an airplane?" I was a little surprised by the question as I have never in all my life had someone ask me if I wanted to buy an airplane. So I asked what kind of plane it was, and it was the exact plane I had sown my seed for. Okay, this had my attention. I went and looked at the plane, contacted the owner, and he took me on a flight. It was perfect. There was only one problem. At the time, I did not have the money to pay for it. But God had a plan.

You see, in the previous fall, and it was now March, I had obtained a house from my father that I was going to rehab into an office building in the spring. Well, my dad told me that he had turned off the water before winter, so I never checked it. Just a few days after I looked at the plane, my brother called and said my house was ruined. He then went on to tell me that all the drywall in the house had been ruined and most of it had fallen off the walls. Apparently, the water was not turned off and had frozen in the winter. Now that it was March and warming up, the water began running in the house and ran for who knows how long, at least a few weeks.

What my brother did not know was that I had already signed

a contract with a building company to strip the entire house of its drywall and the outside siding. This was part of the rebuilding process to convert the house into my new office complex. Now, here is where the cool thing happened. The insurance company paid a claim for the water damage, and that was the cash that I used to pay for my airplane. The plane was purchased with cash!

So remember, partnership is a powerful spiritual principle you will want to be aware of and take advantage of.

This ends our discussion on releasing your seed when you are in faith. So now that you have sowed your seed, what happens next? Trust me, most people do not know, as evidenced by so many Christians who sow but see no return or effect from their giving. Is this the time to sit around drinking lemonade until your harvest comes in?

You had better not! We will discuss what you should be doing in the next chapter.

CHAPTER 8
YOU NEED A PLAN!

When Brad and Charity first came to our church, I really did not know them. I remember saying hello to them and just some small talk from time to time. The first time they caught my attention spiritually was at Drenda's women's conference. The conference started on Thursday night and ended on Saturday afternoon. A lot of the attendees would then stay over for our Saturday evening church service. It was at this service that Brad and Charity came up after service with a request. They wanted to start a business and asked if I would receive a seed into our ministry and pray over them for this business.

I found out later that Charity had rented a booth at the women's conference to sell some of her handmade hair treatments for African-American curly hair. She had rented the table at the conference for $150, and she sold $350 worth of product, which netted her $200.

At the Saturday evening service, they both came forward with the $200 and wanted to sow it into our ministry as a seed for their business to grow. I said, "Of course," and we prayed. I did not think that much about it, but I could see the passion in their eyes, and I could tell they were in faith as they released their seed.

To give you a little background on Brad and Charity, at the time, Brad was an IT manager for a company, and Charity was making $10 per hour part-time, just your average paycheck to paycheck family. After the conference, they continued to sell their product to friends and some online sales but admitted that the business was not really taking off. But God was working behind the scenes preparing their future growth.

Ostrich oil was a major component in their formula, which they purchased from an ostrich farmer in California, who they found out wanted to sell the company. The price was $40,000. Charity knew this was a great opportunity for the future growth of their company, but Brad and Charity did not have the $40,000, none of it. They had enough money for the airline tickets to go and see the company in California, but that was all. Brad said as he got closer to California, the more nervous he got. What would he say to the owner since they had no money and promised each other they would not borrow any money for their business? When they got to California, the farmer showed them all around but told them that he had already found a buyer for the oil company. It looked like things were not working out. But the owner asked Brad to do some IT work for him, which Brad accepted.

During that time, Brad and Charity developed a relationship with the owner; and one day, he said that he had decided to sell the business to them. He ended up taking payments for the business, and Brad and Charity had their ostrich oil company. It was about this time that Brad and Charity heard of a building project we launched at Faith Life Church, and something just jumped on the inside of them. They had seen the first seed they had sown earlier completely change their business, and now they knew it was time to take the business to the next level with a significant seed. Again, Brad and Charity met me at the front of the church and sowed for their business with a seed and a goal they were sowing for. They were not sowing for their personal money but for a six-figure goal they wanted to give to the building project.

To make a long story short, a major change occurred again in the product, and God provided a new ingredient that changed the product so it was the perfect product for African-American curly hair. The product took off. And in no time, they had given the building project that six-figure check. Now, they are supporting projects all over Africa, and their cash flow is more than seven figures. All of this happened within a three-year period of time. What an incredible story of going from $10 per hour to millions in three years! Wow!

This is a great story and a perfect example of how God works with you to capture your provision and to build your influence. The first thing that stood out to me was their hearts for the Kingdom and the purpose for their company, which is to financially support the Kingdom of God. Secondly, it was how they worked with God to develop the structure, product, and plan for the company from basically nothing. This should inspire anyone who wants to do something significant that it is not determined by how much money you have or what you know when you start. God will work with you all along the way.

This brings me to the fourth Kingdom principle that God taught me, and that is after you sow and release your faith, you need to listen for the plan.

Step #4: After You Sow and Release Your Faith, You Need a Plan.

"You yourselves give them something to eat," Jesus answered.

They asked, "Do you want us to go and spend two hundred silver coins on bread in order to feed them?"

So Jesus asked them, "How much bread do you have? Go and see."

When they found out, they told him, "Five loaves and also two fish."

<u>*Jesus then told his disciples to make all the people divide into groups and sit down on the green grass. So the people sat down in rows, in groups of a hundred and groups of fifty. Then Jesus took the five loaves and the two fish, looked up to heaven, and gave thanks to God. He broke the loaves and gave them to his disciples to distribute to the people. He also divided the two fish among them all.*</u> *Everyone ate and had enough. Then the disciples took up twelve baskets full of what was left of the bread and the fish. The number of men who were fed was five thousand.*

—Mark 6:37-44 (GNT)

Jesus gave the disciples a plan of execution <u>before</u> the fish and bread multiplied. So, make sure you understand this. Once you sow your seed in faith, you need to get the plan from the Holy Spirit. The best way to do this is to spend time praying in the Spirit. You do not want to make any decisions or launch out in your own strength until you hear from God. There are several reasons why. First, you will try to do this in your own strength and think way too small. Second, you might try

ONCE YOU SOW YOUR SEED IN FAITH, YOU NEED TO GET THE PLAN FROM THE HOLY SPIRIT.

to build a plan around what you already know when God may want to lead you in a new direction. You have already tried what you know, and you need a fresh idea and plan to change your harvest. So, wait on the Lord for fresh ideas and a plan. It may come from anywhere. You may see an ad, meet a person, or simply have a dream like I did. God will get your attention and help you formulate your new plan. Let me give you an example of why this is so important.

The Power of a Plan

I have probably told this same example in every one of my "Your Financial Revolution" books, but it bears repeating again. If I told you that I could solve all of your financial problems in the next few words, I am sure you would sit up for the details, pen in hand. Well, get ready because here is your answer. Make $10 million net income this year. Yes, I said make $10 million net income before the year is out. For most people, this would set their finances on a good path of solvency.

What? Do I discern a snicker out there? Are you laughing? When I tell people in my audiences to do this, I hear snickers all over the auditorium. I then ask why they are laughing. They are laughing because to them that is a joke; it is not possible. Then I tell them that at some point, as I bring the income goal lower for the year, they will stop laughing and say, "Oh, I can do that."

So, where do you stop laughing, $600,000 a year? Where do you see yourself, $200,000 or $100,000 a year? Maybe your number is much less, maybe $45,000 a year. Somewhere between $10 million and $0 a year, you will find a number where you will say, "I think I can do that." And there is the problem; that's exactly where you will stay. Understand this, no one attempts anything they think is impossible for them. So, here is the problem. You are tied or limited by your own thoughts.

Now, let me show you the power of a plan. Let's take the same statement, that all your financial problems would be solved if you made $10 million net this year. But this time, I am going to offer you a contract to make some money. I am going to pay you $500 a box to put a ball in it, tape it shut, mark it for mailing, and then set it aside. Let's assume you can do 100 boxes an hour, or $50,000 an hour in income. Let's also assume you work a steady 10 hours a day making $500,000 a day in income. Now, when I say let's make $10 million before the year ends, what would you say? "EASY! That would only take 20 days of work." Okay, let me ask you what changed. Nothing except now you have a plan that, if followed, basically guarantees that you will make your goal of $10 million a year in income.

Got it? If left to your own imagination, you probably would have never thought your goal was possible, and you would have settled for whatever YOU thought was possible. But you do not need your opinion; you have already been living in that limited world for far too long. No, you need the Holy Spirit to help you dream.

God Has a Plan For You

I told you earlier in the book of our horrible financial situation and the panic attacks and depression I suffered from due to finances. When I began to learn the Kingdom way of living life, I had nowhere to turn but God. He spoke to me and gave me a plan to start Forward Financial Group and show people how to get out of debt. That is nuts! I remember sitting in my house at the time thinking about what He was telling me to do and wondering to myself, "Boy, I wish you would tell me first." But He answered back that I would walk out of debt as I walked out the plan.

As Drenda and I launched out on the plan that God gave us, we had no equipment, no computer, nothing. But when we saw the plan, I knew it would work; I knew it was possible. And by the plan, I mean the strategy and details He showed us in regard to launching the plan. I could do that! In fact, I would love to do that.

Just like in Brad and Charity's case, God provided all of the start-up equipment we needed. Strangely, one day, my dad, who owned a pizza shop and did not need a computer, told me that he wanted to buy a computer, and he invited me along. So we went and bought his computer and a word processing program that he said I could use on it. Understand, I knew nothing about computers. He lived a mile down the street from me, and I began to play around with that computer and program until I could write up a great client presentation on how to eliminate their debt. God made a way when I did not have money.

The company grew, and I began to hire sales reps. In those days, we would use our handheld financial calculators to work through all the math on each family's plan. We would then type that data into the template, which I had created on my word processing software, to print out for our reps to take back to their clients' home. The dot matrix printer would be singing all day (you do remember those, right?) Soon my secretary could not keep up, and I had to hire another person to help type and print off these client reports.

I realized that I needed a better way to do business. I needed a computer program that could calculate all of the financial equations that needed to be computed in each client's case as well as print it out. Drenda and I asked the Lord for help and that He would provide a computer programmer we could afford to write the entire program for our company.

A couple of months after this prayer, I was on a routine client visit when the client asked me, after seeing the printout I had done for him, "Do you do this by hand?" I said, "Yes, but we are really wanting to move this to a computer program that will do it for us." He looked at me and explained that he wrote computer programs full time at work but would love to help us out by doing one for us in the evening on his own time. He presented a price, and he would allow me to pay as I could over the next year.

That program changed everything and allowed me to hire more people. Soon, we had 300 reps in most of the eastern United States, which caused our office to become the number one office out of 5,000 offices for one of our venders.

By launching our own company and following the Holy Spirit, we became completely debt free, and the rest is history, as they say. What I am saying is God will give you the plan if you will ask Him and let Him do it. He will take you places you never thought possible.

So, let me emphasize that you need the plan. God has a plan for your success. In fact, He has many plans for your success. His ideas and wisdom are endless.

> *"For I know the plans I have for you" declares the Lord, "plans to prosper you and not to harm you, plans to give you hope and a future."*
>
> —Jeremiah 29:11

How Do You Hear the Plan of God?

So, how do you hear the plan? As I said, praying in the Spirit is the best way to hear. I am not going to cover praying in the Spirit at great length here because my book *Your Financial Revolution: The Power of Strategy* covers hearing the Holy Spirit in great detail. But a brief notation is warranted.

> *We do, however, speak a message of wisdom among the mature, but not the wisdom of this age or of the rulers of this age, who are coming to nothing. No, we declare God's wisdom, a mystery that has been hidden and that God destined for our glory before time began. None of the rulers of this age understood it, for if they had, they would not have crucified the Lord of glory.*
>
> *However, as it is written: "<u>What no eye has seen, what no ear has heard, and what no human mind has conceived</u>"—<u>the things God has prepared for those who love him</u>—these are the things God has revealed to us by his Spirit.*
>
> *The Spirit searches all things, even the deep things of God. For who knows a person's thoughts except their own spirit within them? In the same way no one knows the thoughts of God except the Spirit of God. What we have received is not the spirit of the world, but the Spirit who is from God, so that we may understand what God has freely given us.*
>
> —1 Corinthians 2:6-12

The things we have not heard, seen, or thought of, as mentioned in this Scripture, are the things that are revealed to us by the Holy Spirit. Sounds like a great benefit to me; I could use that. When you became a Christian, the Holy Spirit came to dwell in you, and He began to lead your life.

But there is another dimension of the Holy Spirit that Jesus gave the church, called the baptism of the Holy Spirit. This is what we see take place on the Day of Pentecost when the Holy Spirit came on the disciples in the upper room just as He came upon Jesus at the River Jordan. This is when Jesus began His ministry. This is when the power of God came on Him to be a witness of the Kingdom. Jesus did no miracles as a child. He did not multiply His family's food or walk on water. To understand the baptism of the Holy Spirit, you will need to understand that there is a difference between being born again (when the Spirit of God comes in you) and the baptism of the Holy Spirit (when the Holy Spirit comes upon you.)

> *On the evening of that first day of the week, when the disciples were together, with the doors locked for fear of the Jewish leaders, Jesus came and stood among them and said, "Peace be with you!" After he said this, he showed them his hands and side. The disciples were overjoyed when they saw the Lord.*
>
> *Again Jesus said, "Peace be with you! As the Father has sent me, I am sending you." And with that he breathed on them and said, "Receive the Holy Spirit."*
>
> —John 20:19-22

The disciples were born again right there in John 20, yet Jesus told them that they still had to wait upon this baptism of the Holy Spirit which would enable them to be witnesses of the Kingdom of God.

After his suffering, he presented himself to them and gave many convincing proofs that he was alive. He appeared to them over a period of forty days and spoke about the kingdom of God. On one occasion, while he was eating with them, he gave them this command: "Do not leave Jerusalem, but wait for the gift my Father promised, which you have heard me speak about. For John baptized with water, but in a few days you will be baptized with the Holy Spirit."

—Acts 1:3-5

But you will receive power when the Holy Spirit <u>comes on you</u>; and you will be my witnesses in Jerusalem, and in all Judea and Samaria, and to the ends of the earth.

—Acts 1:8

This anointing from God brings the power of God and enables you to do His works. Please notice that it comes on you and not in you. You may also remember that on the Day of Pentecost all of the disciples who had been waiting in Jerusalem in the upper room were baptized with the Holy Spirit. What was one of the evidences of this? They all spoke in tongues. Speaking in tongues is listed in 1 Corinthians 12 as one of the nine spiritual gifts that were given to the church. You may say that those gifts passed away, but I strongly disagree. The baptism of the Holy Spirit brings with it all nine spiritual gifts, but I want to focus on just this one gift, speaking in tongues.

THIS ANOINTING FROM GOD BRINGS THE POWER OF GOD AND ENABLES YOU TO DO HIS WORKS.

At first, this may sound useless since you may think it is only needed if you are speaking to people who speak a different language and you are trying to preach the Gospel. But being able to speak to people in a language that you do not know was never the intent of the gift of speaking in tongues. Let me show you why it is an invaluable gift and why it is important to your prosperity.

> *For anyone who speaks in a tongue does not speak to people but to God. Indeed, no one understands them; they utter mysteries by the Spirit. But the one who prophesies speaks to people for their strengthening, encouraging and comfort. <u>Anyone who speaks in a tongue edifies themselves</u>, but the one who prophesies edifies the church. <u>I would like every one of you to speak in tongues</u>, but I would rather have you prophesy. The one who prophesies is greater than the one who speaks in tongues unless someone interprets, so that the church may be edified.*
>
> —1 Corinthians 14:2-5

We need to understand the context of Paul's letter here. He is speaking about how a church gathering should be conducted. He is basically saying that speaking in tongues does no good to those who hear it in the church service because those who hear it do not understand what the person is saying. Paul says in the church it is more profitable to prophesy since that would be in the common language of the people and be more effective.

But when it comes to an individual praying in tongues, wow, that is a different story. Speaking in tongues has a great benefit to the one who speaks. The Bible says they are uttering mysteries through their spirits. These mysteries are what you don't know and what you need to know. Secondly, Paul says that the person who speaks in a tongue edifies himself. The word edify means to bring instruction. Obviously, if you need to know something, it is a mystery to you at that moment. But speaking in tongues brings instruction to the one speaking. You and I need that for sure if we are going to develop plans that are beyond what we already know. As 1 Corinthians 2:9-10 say:

What no eye has seen, what no ear has heard, and what no human mind has conceived—the things God has prepared for those who love him—these are the things God has revealed to us by his Spirit.

I need that help, and so do you. Your next question is, "If you are speaking in tongues and you do not understand what you are saying, then how do you gain anything from what you are saying?" Well, here is the mystery. As the Holy Spirit is speaking through your own human spirit, your mind begins to pick up some of the thoughts that are flowing through you. We call this revelation, and the word comes from the root of to reveal. So, by praying in the Spirit, as speaking in tongues is called in the Bible, you have the ability to pick up on ideas and thoughts that are not your own.

I know you probably have a ton of questions about this, so let me encourage you to get my book *Your Financial Revolution: The Power of Strategy*. You will find all your answers there.

Pause and Pray for Strategy

For now, let's just understand that once you sow your seed in faith, the next step is to stop and pray in the Holy Spirit for a while because you need a plan. This is what Karla did.

Karla and Todd were living the normal American lifestyle, paycheck to paycheck and falling further and further into debt. Karla had spotted the *Fixing the Money Thing* broadcast one day on TV and knew that she needed to get their finances in order. I can remember the email that I received from Karla. At the time, she said that they had no financial plan. They could not even see a couple of months ahead, they were so tight. Any shortages in their budget were covered by credit cards.

She knew that they needed to get out of debt, but how? She and her husband sowed a seed for a business idea after reading my book, and they sowed explicitly for a business that she could do from home. Todd was already busy as a school teacher at the local school, so she was wondering what she could do to help. Every morning after they sowed for an idea, Karla would have some quiet time with the Lord, waiting to hear some direction from the Holy Spirit.

One morning, up out of her spirit, she heard the word puppies. At first she was a little confused. Puppies? Raise puppies? They once had a dog, but raising puppies was something that she had not really thought of. When Todd came home that evening, she wanted to tell him what God had said. As expected, Todd was a little apprehensive of the plan but encouraged Karla to explore the possibilities. Soon Todd and Karla bought two female goldendoodle puppies and started their little puppy business. Of course, they had to raise their puppies first and then begin the breeding process.

There were a few setbacks along the way, but the first year their dogs had pups, it had 13. The dogs sold for around $1,500 each, and Karla says she was in tears as she realized that she had heard the Holy Spirit correctly when she heard the word puppies. In that same year, Todd was also promoted to the position of principal at the local school.

The puppy business continued to grow; and at this point in time, they have had over 300 puppies, and the price has gone up to around

$2,500 each. Their financial life has done a 180! They paid their house off last year and are now completely out of debt. They have traveled out of the country on amazing trips and have seen God do so much in their family that Karla just had to tell people about His Kingdom. She has just released her first book, *Plans to Prosper: How God Gave Us Financial Freedom Through Puppies*.

Todd and Karla are living the Kingdom lifestyle, one which catches people's attention and causes them to stop and think of God. The prophet Isaiah spoke of the church age in Isaiah 61 where he told us what God wants to do with our lives while we are on the earth.

> *They will be called oaks of righteousness, a planting of the Lord for the display of his splendor.*
> —Isaiah 61:3

An oak is a very sturdy tree and usually is massive in size as well. The Bible says our lives will be like oak trees, anchored, steadfast, and immovable. The fruit of this tree will be righteousness, which simply means people will see what life is supposed to look like, what God calls right. We are plantings of the Lord, which means God is going to set us where He sees fit, all in various places, of all occupations and cultures, to display His splendor. God wants to catch people's attention with you! He wants people to see the good fruit of His ways in your life. Just as a fruit tree draws you toward it with its delectable fruit, God wants your life to look like heaven on Earth.

So how did Todd and Karla do it? Of course, it took a lot of work to raise those puppies, but the freedom was certainly worth it. That freedom all started by hearing the plan, a word from God. One simple word is all she heard, "Puppies!" But that was all that was needed. God will speak to you as well. He will lead you to those green pastures and the still waters of peace that Psalm 23 talks about.

But as you can imagine, just hearing the plan is not enough. I am going to discuss step 5 in the next chapter, and it may well be the most important chapter of them all because step 5 is where most people fail. But not you, you are going to walk in the goodness of God just like the stories you have read in this book! Are you ready? Let's move on to step number 5.

CHAPTER 9
IT'S TIME TO GO!

Every farmer knows that every harvest has a unique and specific timing attached to it. Knowing the correct harvest season for a particular crop is the difference between success and failure. And let's be very clear: you can miss the harvest. So, this is a very big and important topic. Have you ever been to the store, seen this great looking red apple, and thought, *That is a great looking apple*—but when you got home and took a bite then thought, *Wow, this thing has no flavor*? Well, that is a timing issue.

I cannot tell you how many financial disasters I have heard of and dealt with from people jumping out into an idea and missing the timing. My favorite Scripture concerning timing is Matthew 13:44.

> *The kingdom of heaven is like **treasure** hidden in a field. When a man found it, he hid it again, and then in his joy went and sold all he had and bought that field.*

In this story, the man was wise enough to know that at that minute, he was not capable of actually owning the treasure. He had to go and prepare to purchase it.

As an example, when Karla heard the word puppies, it did not mean she was to put out her shingle advertising puppies for sale. She didn't have any puppies yet. There was a lot of preparation to do. They had to buy their two female dogs first. They had to build a place to house them and plan for the puppies that were to come. There were legal issues that had to be learned regarding required vaccines that puppies must have if you are going to sell them.

There are also the issues of licensing, marketing, banking, and taxes, to mention a few. These things need to be looked into before you actually step into the harvest season of your business idea.

Assuming you have done your due diligence, the hard part is still ahead. You have to step out into the vision that God has spoken to you. Yes, the idea will be bigger than you, and there may be some fear involved in stepping out. But fear was the old you. Remember, this is the new you.

When God spoke to me regarding launching out into my own business, I was really nervous about it. I was starting totally from scratch. Even though God spoke to me in a dream to step out and I had done the due diligence, I was still nervous about it. Everything now hinged on me actually stepping out and doing it. Have you ever had a friend or knew a person that was always talking about what they were going to do but never doing it? I have known a lot of them! Remember, I have trained salesmen for over 30 years.

When I launched my business, I had no leads given to me. I was living strictly on commissions, and I was a one-man operation. But one thing I did have was passion. When God led me to start a company to help people get out of debt, I was all in. I had been tormented with financial issues for most of my life; and now that I had found the answer, the Kingdom of God, I wanted to tell everyone about it. Secondly, once God helped me put the plan together that showed me how to produce written plans for families to get out of debt in five to seven years, including their home mortgages and without changing their budgets, I was beyond passionate. I knew I had a niche in the financial market, and I had a story to tell. But again, I had to have the prototype already fine-tuned before I turned on the switch.

Sure there are always things you learn along the way, but when you jump, you should have the basic structure already developed. But no matter how great the opportunity, the product, or the potential paycheck, it is always today, and today is the day that you must step into the plan.

Now, this brings me to the real problem, what I believe is the main reason that so many do not reach their goals, even after they have heard from God regarding the direction and answer for their financial issues.

Procrastination!

Procrastination can be based in insecurity, fear, or just laziness. But one thing is for sure; it is easy to do! I read the following study concerning grad students' habits in regard to procrastination.

Jenny cleans her apartment. Cathy does math puzzles. Matt checks sports scores, and Carmen updates her Facebook page. All of them are psychology students putting off other tasks they're supposed to be doing. Classic procrastination in action.

It's a tough habit to break, particularly these days when the Internet allows students to escape disciplined study time with the click of a mouse. A 2007 meta-analysis by University of Calgary psychologist Piers Steel, PhD, reports that 80 percent to

95 percent of college students procrastinate, particularly when it comes to doing their coursework.[6]

Well, I would suggest that this does not only apply to grad students. The distractions are intense. Picking up my phone or opening emails are sure time killers. But procrastination has a more subtle, demonic side that you need to be aware of. To illustrate and to shed light on this dangerous topic—yes, I said dangerous—I want to go to 1 Corinthians 2:6-8.

*We do, however, speak a message of wisdom among the mature, but not the wisdom of this age or of the rulers of this age, who are coming to nothing. No, we declare God's wisdom, a mystery that has been hidden and that God destined for our glory before time began. **None of the rulers of this age understood it, for if they had, they would not have crucified the Lord of glory**.*

—1 Corinthians 2:6-8

Wow, you had better write this down somewhere. Satan will change tactics if he can figure out what you are doing! This is why God speaks in parables. This is why God waits until the midnight hour sometimes before He reveals your answer. You must know and remember that we have an enemy. Your enemy is not just a figurative character with a pitchfork and a red costume. The Bible is clear:

Be alert and of sober mind. Your enemy the devil prowls around like a roaring lion looking for someone to devour.

—Peter 5:8

6 https://www.apa.org/gradpsych/2010/01/procrastination

Now, of course he cannot just devour anyone, but he wants to pull you outside of heaven's jurisdiction into his legal dominion to kill, steal, and destroy. The Bible says, "Your enemy!" One of Satan's tactics is to lure you into complacency, into a place of procrastination. This will give him time to figure out what you and God are up to.

I remember a dream I had one night. The picture that I saw was at night, and the light from my bedroom window was cast out upon the lawn until it faded into the darkness. There just where the light faded, in the shadows, I saw two demons standing facing my window with notebooks in their hands. I knew they were **PROCRASTINATION CAN BE DEADLY!** sent to find a legal opening into my home. They were taking notes, looking for a place of weakness with which they would attempt to stop the work of God.

Procrastination can be deadly! That sounds strong, doesn't it? It sounds exactly the opposite of what the temptation of procrastination says to you. His voice is subtle and convincing, "It won't matter if you do it later." You can always do it later. But is that true? Let me share a story that will show you just how dangerous procrastination can be.

> *Meanwhile, the Philistine, with his shield bearer in front of him, kept coming closer to David. He looked David over and saw that he was little more than a boy, glowing with health and handsome, and he despised him. He said to David, "Am I a dog, that you come at me with sticks?" And the Philistine cursed David by his gods. "Come here," he said, "and I'll give your flesh to the birds and the wild animals!"*
>
> —1 Samuel 17:41-44

As the Philistine moved closer to attack him, David ran quickly toward the battle line to meet him. Reaching into his bag and taking out a stone, he slung it and struck the Philistine on the forehead. The stone sank into his forehead, and he fell facedown on the ground.

—1 Samuel 17:48-49

The story of David and Goliath is such an awesome story. The entire nation of Israel is in fear as they hear Goliath's rants. But David says he will fight him with one condition: he can choose his own weapon, a sling which he has used for years while guarding the sheep. As David approaches Goliath, Goliath is confused and yelling out." "Am I a dog, that you come at me with sticks?" What Goliath thinks is a stick is actually David's staff. He does not see the sling tucked under his belt. No, David is using the staff as a decoy, drawing Goliath's attention to it instead of to the sling. As Goliath advances toward David, David runs toward Goliath. This was another tactic David used. He knew it would be much harder for Goliath to see the sling if he moved on him suddenly.

But what if David had acted like many people do? Fearful to enter the conflict, they simply procrastinate. What if David had danced around Goliath until he felt ready to make his move? I believe that Goliath would have seen the sling, recognized David's strategy, and compensated accordingly. The battle would have been lost and the entire nation of Israel taken captive.

THIS IS EXACTLY WHAT SATAN WANTS TO DO WITH YOU. HE WANTS TO TAKE YOUR PLANS CAPTIVE.

This is exactly what Satan wants to do with you. He wants to take your plans captive. If he can cause you to pause, to wait until you feel ready, he will have time to change his tactic to counter the plan of God in your life. So is procrastination dangerous? Absolutely! I am sure that it has already cost you thousands of dollars in your life. In David's case, it could have cost thousands of lives.

This is why, when you know the timing and you have your plan, step out with confidence. I believe you will have a prompting from the Holy Spirit to help you know when things are right to step out. But because of wrong teaching, many hesitate or step out and then, when they find conflict, they step back and think they must have missed God.

Do Not Fear the Conflict

People tell me that when they stepped out, all hell broke out. Well, you have been equipped to handle hell with no fear. The enemy has just been slammed with your Holy Spirit plan, and he is reacting to shut it down. He cannot stop it now. It is too late. But if he can get you to doubt the word of the Lord that led you here, then fear will drive you back. He wants to cause such a ruckus that you back down. But you need to stand strong now more than ever and use your authority to keep him in check. Do not be afraid to say, "No, you will not do that" or "I bind that spirit of confusion which is trying to torment me. I know what the Lord said to do, and I am doing it, in Jesus's name. Now back off, Satan!"

Unfortunately, most of today's untrained Christians react to Satan's counterattack with surprise. They believe that since God has spoken to them and has given them His plan that everything is going to go smoothly and quickly with no surprises.

Now, do not misunderstand what I am saying. We have absolute authority over evil spirits, but we do not have absolute authority over people. It is to be noted that although I am under God's jurisdiction, many people around me are not and will fall prey to rumors and confusion. They may misjudge my motives or bring persecution against me.

But they cannot stop your Holy Spirit plan!!! The enemy will continue to come up a day late and a dollar short. God is way ahead of them and will lead you to your victory if you stay strong in faith and refuse to compromise.

The stepping out phase is the phase where it will take more courage than faith to walk it out. Faith brought you to this moment, but now it will take courage to step out. I think the problem is that people get the Red Sea story and the Jordan River story confused.

In the Red Sea story, the people of Israel have been delivered out of Egypt and have traveled to the Red Sea where they appear to be hemmed in by the sea and mountains as Pharaoh has changed his mind and is coming after them. It seems there is no way of escape. But Moses raises his staff (authority), and the Red Sea parts. They cross over on dry land, and Pharaoh's army tries to follow. But as Pharaoh's army does so, the sea engulfs them, killing all of them. Israel is now free from Egypt and free from slavery. This is a mighty act of deliverance, and we all love to sing of God's deliverance.

Ahead is their promise, the land of Canaan. It is the land of their forefathers and has been promised to Abraham's seed. As they travel through the desert, the words of Moses ring in their ears: it will be a land that flows with milk and honey. It sounds too good to be true to the people who have only known slavery their entire lives. But there is a problem. The land is already occupied by other nations. As they approach the River Jordan, Moses decides to send out spies to check the best route for them to travel once they cross over into the new land and to bring back some of its fruit to prove to the people that it is a good land full of potential.

But the spies bring back a story that makes the nation of Israel want to head back to Egypt. The land is filled with walled cities and people who are much bigger and taller than the Israelites. The Israelites weep with discouragement and turn on God and Moses, thinking they have been lied to. Because of their unbelief, God does not lead them into the promise as He knows that without faith, they will be destroyed. That generation lives and dies in the desert until none of that generation is left.

Now, Joshua is commanded by God to lead them across. But again, as they come to the Jordan River, there is a problem. The river is at the flood stage, and the people cannot cross the fast-moving water. But God once more splits the waters, and the Israelites walk across the dry land—this time not from conflict, as it was when they left Egypt, but into conflict as they prepare to capture their promise.

This is what you must know. There could be issues or problems to solve as you step out, but do not fear. God will help you and protect you as you do. Always remember that right behind that problem is the promise. Never forget that.

In fact, I am going to say something here that may shock you. Be problem conscious. No, I am not talking about you meditating on your personal problems in fear. I am talking about you looking for an opportunity. You see, people pay big money to clean up or fix problems. A business is really an answer to someone's problem. As an example, people have a problem—they are hungry—so someone starts a Subway shop. I am sure you probably have made a sub sandwich before, but you did not translate that into a business concept. But today, Subway has tens of thousands of stores all over the planet because they are solving someone's problem. And you will say, "I could have done that," and you could have. But you need to think differently.

Drenda and I are millionaires today, not because we are smart or are good-looking. We simply learned how the Kingdom of God operates, and God showed us how to fix a problem that we had. Then God showed us how to help other people solve the same problem. It is not that difficult!

The Place of Preparation

So, after you sow in faith and after you get the plan, do not just jump out without thinking. Remember our Scripture in Matthew 13.

> *The kingdom of heaven is like treasure hidden in a field. When a man found it, he hid it again, and then in his joy went and sold all he had and bought that field.*
>
> —Matthew 13:44

God always calls you to a place of preparation first. So even though you hear from God and He has given you an idea that is going to start a fantastic new business, be sure of the timing. God always reveals the treasure to motivate you toward preparation first. Notice I did not say God gives you the treasure. I said He reveals the treasure, the answer. Many, many people have misread the revelation of the treasure as the time to capture the treasure, with horrible results. God will always lead you into a place of training and preparation before He sends you out to occupy the treasure.

I know in my case as a young man, God gave me a vision of me standing and holding a Bible in my hand. While standing there, I not only saw me preaching from the Bible but I also saw the room and the people that I was preaching to. A voice spoke to me as I saw that vision. "I am calling you to preach My Word." I heard that three times then the vision vanished. I was 19 years old. I was running my dad's pizza shop at the time and really did not know what the vision meant entirely. I did know that I was called to preach God's Word, but how or where that would take place I did not know yet.

In reality, that was a call of preparation. It was not that much longer after God gave me that revelation that He told me to go to a Bible school and then on to ORU. There I met the love of my life, Drenda. We went on from ORU to start a financial business, a plan that I just did not understand at the time. What happened to the call of God on my life? But God had a plan. He used that time to train me in the financial areas of life, to train me in His Kingdom laws and principles, which have become the cornerstone of my ministry. He also used that time to help me grow in self-confidence as I was so afraid to talk to people when I was younger.

It wasn't until September 1st, 1995 that God led us to launch our church in the basement of a local Christian radio station. Our first service was at night, and as I stood there, I saw the exact picture of that vision that God had given me 21 years earlier.

So understand that when you hear the vision, get the direction, or get the idea, that usually does not mean to jump out at that moment. God will tell you when to step out the same way He gave you the plan. He will speak to you, and you will know it.

In my case, we were attending a small church close to our home in 1995; and in a Sunday night service, God began to deal with me. I could not even hear what the pastor was saying as the Spirit of God was on me so strongly. I knew it was time to step out! And you will too.

Drenda and I have so loved seeing all that God has done, but our passion is all that He is doing!!!!! We have committed ourselves to preach and teach this message of the Kingdom for the rest of our lives. Nothing thrills us more than to see people's faces light up with revelation when we teach. We know what that means; they are hearing answers.

We know that the Kingdom is your answer too! So what is the fifth principle that God taught me?

Step #5: When you know the timing, method, and place, don't procrastinate! Secondly, do not be surprised by the conflict.

You and God can get the job done, no doubt about it! Just remember that it is God's will that you prosper.

> *Beloved, I pray that in all respects you may prosper and be in good health, just as your soul prospers.*
>
> —3 John 2 (NASB)

Do not let anyone tell you that it is not God's will and His best for you to be healthy and to prosper in life! This is what Satan stole from the earth realm and what God has restored to you in Jesus Christ. Religion has taught people such lies about God. Sometimes people need to unlearn fiction before they can learn the truth. I received the following email the other day, which illustrates the need to renew your mind to what God really says.

Dear Gary,

My name is Annette. I grew up in a Baptist pastor's home, was saved as a child, and loved Jesus immensely. As a young adult, I was baptized in the Holy Spirit and began to understand true worship, healing, deliverance, spiritual gifts, and other truths about the Kingdom of God. I learned the basic principles of sowing and reaping through various teachers in the body of Christ. But it was not until my husband, John, "stumbled" across your teachings that I began to realize that I had a real problem believing that Christians—especially pastors and or people in ministry—should seek to prosper beyond having their basic needs met. We discovered that neither of us really understood how God's Kingdom works.

We were in the ministry and were faithful to tithe. We were also generous givers and even taught the principle of sowing and reaping. But we felt that we lived relatively comfortable lives and that was all we should expect. That was until the fall of 2003 when we had a bad fire at our dock where we had our business and ministry headquartered. Then several other events happened that changed everything. John began having continual heart issues, eventually needing open heart surgery. We did not have health insurance at the time, and we began to incur large hospital bills. His inability to work made things even worse. And then some bad decisions on our part caused greater financial issues. By 2015, our normal financial lifestyle had changed from being pretty good to that of being burdened with large debt, including back taxes.

We have always been generous because we love to give and believe in sowing and reaping. We desperately sought the Lord more than ever for answers. Then John stumbled across your teaching on TV. At first he said, "You can't buy God like that" and turned the TV off. But a few days later, he came across your program again, and that time he couldn't stop listening. He ended up ordering every teaching tool you had available at that time! We fed on that material for two years before we both were able to let go of the crazy belief that it was wrong to want to have an abundance and more than enough.

One day, we were watching, for about the tenth time, a particular DVD where you teach from Matthew 17 about Jesus telling Peter to catch a fish and to use the coin in its mouth to pay the taxes, along with an illustration from 2 Kings 4 about the woman who used what she had in her house.

I suddenly remembered that a few years ago a friend had given us a gold coin in exchange for some work we had done for them. It was not enough to pay off our debt, but it was the "something" we had in our house that we could sow! We sowed that coin into your ministry and became an Inner Circle Partner and watched to see what God would do next.

Over the next couple of months, we continued to feed on your teachings, and we struggled to keep our heads above water while making payments on the debt. Then one night, I had a dream in which God showed me a large sum of money was coming to us. During the weeks that followed, we saw a few small financial blessings trickle in. We continued to pray and give more as God directed, and we declared God's truths and listened to make sure we obeyed everything we believed He was telling us to do.

Then a situation reversed that had seemed almost impossible to happen. We saw the fulfillment of the dream come to pass shortly thereafter. The amount of money we received was far above and beyond what we needed in order to pay off the debt we owed. We are now out of debt. We are now seeking strategies on how to invest wisely and live the double portion life so that we can give generously, always, and on every occasion.

—John and Annette

We get this kind of email all the time from people who are learning the truth about God and His Kingdom and realizing that they have been lied to by religion.

I found out that once my mind was renewed to God's goodness and His Word, then I was able to grow in the revelation I needed to be free. Remember, never doubt God. If there is a situation in your life that may look like a failure on the part of the Kingdom of God, do what the disciples did. They did not ask Jesus, "Jesus, why didn't you cast that demon out?" No, they asked, "Why couldn't we cast the demon out?" They knew that the short circuit had to be on their end, and they asked Jesus to help them understand it. If you do not see what the Bible says is yours in your life, ask God to show you why! He will speak to you and help you learn how His amazing Kingdom operates.

HE WILL SPEAK TO YOU AND HELP YOU LEARN HOW HIS AMAZING KINGDOM OPERATES.

Just yesterday, a businessman in my church heard from his bank that the federal grant money he was at first promised was declined.

He had already anticipated that money and had made plans for it. Without the help, he would have to lay off his employees. When he asked the bank why the money had been denied, they could not answer why. Since he thought he had plenty of money coming in, he had gone ahead and invested the money he had on the supplies he needed. But now with the money not coming, he found himself out of money and did not know what to do. The only thing he had left was a gift card in his wallet that someone had given him. He immediately drove with it to the church, because he knew he had to sow what he had and believe God to help him in this difficult season. Within hours of dropping the gift card off at the church as a seed, the bank called him and said they were sorry, that there must have been a mistake. They were sending him the money.

You Have a Part to Play

As I close, let me give you my final words concerning capturing the money you need. I found that a lot of God's people have hearts to give, hearts for people, but no money. I believe that the main reason people fail to see a return on their giving is a wrong perception of what is supposed to happen after they give. Many Christians falsely believe that God is just going to bring them the money they believe for. But that is not possible as God has no money. All money is in the earth realm and is only a product of commerce (buying or selling something).

So once we give, if we understand this aspect of the process, we must listen to the Holy Spirit for a plan, a direction, or an idea where we can either create or capture wealth in the marketplace. This does not mean you have to have a business per se, but the Holy Spirit will direct you to someplace in the marketplace to place your net. A net is something that has the ability to catch or create money in the marketplace. God will direct your steps and the plan you are to follow. For most people, I believe the best, fastest, and most likely net is a business. When I say business, I am not excluding working under or in a corporation, but the net needs to be big enough to catch the fish you need. It could be your own or someone else's business.

But when it comes to nets, in my experience, most people are fishing for whales in bathtubs. Let me explain. Let's say someone has a job down at the local grocery store making $10 an hour. But now they desire to pay off their $150,000 house and want to use Kingdom law to accomplish it. Okay, good so far.

Next, they hear about sowing and reaping, a law of the Kingdom, and they sow and believe to pay off that house. Again, good so far. But for some reason, they think that the money is just going to show up. They know that their job does not have the capacity to catch enough money to pay off the house, so they cast their hope on the Lord (and that is good). But when I say "put our hope in the Lord," you need to understand what I am saying is that we are putting our hope in the Lord to give us wisdom and direction to capture that money. And that may mean major changes are involved.

You see, what people fail to realize is that God may need to direct them to a new lake to catch a whale, not their familiar bathtub. You see, there are no whales in your bathtub! Paying off a $150,000 house in a couple of years on $10 an hour would be hard to do. But God does know where the fish are and can direct you to the right spot and method to catch the fish you require to reach your goal. Remember the story of Peter and the huge catch of fish? Peter had fished all night and caught nothing, but Jesus told him where to fish; and afterward, Peter's boat could not hold all the fish. The difference? A word of direction, "Drop your nets in the deep water." You see, Peter was fishing in the wrong place, but Jesus told him what to do and his success changed.

When Drenda and I were in serious debt, we had to learn to hear God and follow Him to bigger and bigger lakes to catch the fish we needed. God's direction kept taking us out to deeper and deeper water. Quite frankly, God led us out so far that we could not see land any longer, which was a very scary place to be since we had never been there before, and especially scary when the storms showed up.

Since most people are waiting on God for the money to appear, it never occurs to them to be listening for something that is foreign to them and is leading them into new and scary places they have never been to before. Most people only look to the familiar, what they already know. But the whales are not in your bathtub. You need to go out to the deep water.

So remember, we are not to sit by idly once we sow. When we do sow, we can hold on to the Word of God and know that God will lead us to the harvest. But we must listen for that direction, follow it, and then have the nets to catch the whales when we get there.

Many people actually take the steps to change lakes but fail to change the methods used to catch their harvest. A bluegill hook will not hold a whale. (By the way, I am not saying we should actually catch whales. I am only using this as an example due to their size.)

Once you are in the correct place, your methods must be able to handle the greater weight and pressure that catching a bigger harvest will require. All of this takes time to put into place. Many times, God knows that we are not capable of handling the whale we are hunting once we come eye to eye with it. But God will train us, and we can be sure that we will indeed haul that catch to shore if we faint not.

So in review, we need to stop thinking in terms of miracle money or what I call a mailbox mentality (although God does some amazing things). Rather, we need to work with God, prepare for the harvest, and do our parts to capture every opportunity that God puts in front of us.

The Power of Provision has been put into your hands. No, I am not talking about the title of my book. I am talking about the Holy Spirit and the Kingdom that God has set you in. So go for it, and win many to Christ by your success and example along the way.

> **WE NEED TO WORK WITH GOD, PREPARE FOR THE HARVEST, AND DO OUR PARTS TO CAPTURE EVERY OPPORTUNITY THAT GOD PUTS IN FRONT OF US.**

Hey, I just saw this email come in, and I thought it was a good reminder as we close.

In the middle of the world economy falling apart, our business just had a $4000 debt and an $8,000 debt wiped out! There's more though!! We were looking at our business finances and realized that, as of today, our business net income for 2020 so far has exceeded our entire business net income for all of 2019! We are prospering above and beyond all we could ask or think (Ephesians 3:20) while the earth cursed world economy is failing! We are just so excited about what God is doing. He is SO faithful to His Word!!

Thank you, thank you, thank you to Gary and Drenda, their family, their staff, and their partners for bringing the Word of God into our lives! We lived for 17 years in poverty and destitution—like Gary and Drenda did for 9 years—until our pastors started showing the Fixing the Money Thing series on Wednesday nights at church. That was 5.5 years ago, and we have never been the same!! Thanks again, and be blessed!

Hey, tell me your stories at GaryKeesee.com. Others need to hear how awesome the Kingdom is working in your life.